The Holy Spirit and Orthodoxy

God, Our Righteousness

~∞~

By
Fidelis A. Olafusi, Kss

ISBN:

Print: 978-1-950320-92-9
Ebook: 978-1-950320-94-3

Contents

CHAPTER 4

The Holy Spirit

~~~

In The Church
"For we are God's co-workers. You are God's field, God's building."

"Do you not know that you are THE TEMPLE OF GOD, and that the Spirit of God dwells in you?" (1Cor. 3: 9, 16 HCSB)

The Apostles' Pentecost Exploits

"When the day of Pentecost had arrived,… Suddenly a sound like that of a violent rushing wind came from heaven… And tongues, like flames of fire… rested on each one of them. Then they were all filled with the Holy Spirit and began to speak in different languages, as the Spirit gave them ability for speech."

"There were Jews living in Jerusalem, devout men from every nation… A crowd came together and was confused because each one heard them speaking in his own language. And they were astounded and amazed saying, "…How is it that each of us can hear in our own native language? Parthians, Medes, Elamites, those who live in Mesopotamia, in Judea and Cappadocia, Pontus and Asia, Phrygia and Pamphylia, Egypt and … Libya… visitors from Rome… Cretans and Arabs – we hear them speaking… in our own languages" "… and that day about 3,000 people were added to them." (Acts 2: 1-11, 41 HCSB)

Acts 5:1–10 Ananias and his wife, Sapphira lied to the Holy Spirit concerning the proceeds of their personal property – they died for it.

Matthias Election: Two chosen – Joseph (also known as Barsabbas and Justus) as well as Matthias. Lot fell on Matthias.

Witnessing by the Holy Spirit – You can't buy the gift of God with money.

Simon, alias the power of God, used to practise magic in Samaria. All were astounded and 'paid attention to him for a long time'.

Philip went down to Samaria and proclaimed the Messiah to them, preaching and baptizing. Simon, himself believed and was baptized and became devoted to Philip when he saw 'the signs and mighty deeds that were occurring'.

Peter and John, who were sent from Jerusalem laid hands on the converts. They received the Holy Spirit.

Commercialising Spiritual Gifts:

"When Simon saw that the Holy Spirit was given through the laying on of the Apostle's hands, he offered them money –" "Give me the power too…" "But Peter told him, 'may your silver be destroyed with you, because you thought the gift of God could be obtained with money'" (Acts 8: 18, 20)

Simon said in reply, 'pray for me to the Lord…'

(For more read this in Acts 8: 8-13, 18-24)

The unforgivable Sin "…I tell you, people will be forgiven every sin and blasphemy, but the **blasphemy against the Spirit** will not be forgiven. Whoever speaks a word against the Son of Man, it will be forgiven him. But whoever speaks against the Holy Spirit, it will not be forgiven him, either in this age or in the one to come". (Matt. 12:31-32 HCSB)

Gifts: Speaking in tongues (usually accompanied with prophesying) –

The Twelve Disciples at Ephesus

"While Apollos was in Corinth, Paul travelled through the interior regions and came to Ephesus. He found some disciples and asked them, 'Did you receive the Holy Spirit when you believed?'

'No,' they told him, 'we haven't even heard that there is a Holy Spirit.'"

"When they heard this, they were baptized in the name of the Lord Jesus. And when Paul had laid his hands on them, the Holy Spirit came on them, and they began to speak in other languages and to prophesy. Now there were about 12 men in all." (Acts 19: 1-2, 5-7 HCSB)

HOLY SPIRIT

Will be poured on all, your old men will have dreams. (Joel 2: 28-29). op cit

Unclean Spirits know who Jesus is as in the healing of the Gerasene demoniac:

"What have You to do with me, Jesus, Son of the Most High God?

I beg You… " (Lk. 8:28 NABRE).

Accomplished by His Spirit

"This is the word of the Lord to Zerubbabel:

'Not by might, and not by power, but by My Spirit, says the Lord of hosts'"

(Zech 4: 6 HCSB)

The sent:

"Who are you, o great mountain? Before Zerubbabel you become a plain…

amid shouts of favour, favour, favour" (Zec. 4: 7 HCSB)

The Spirit gives Life

"The Spirit … gives life. The flesh doesn't … the words that I have spoken to you are Spirit and are Life." (Jn. 6:63)

Ask, get the Holy Spirit

"… If you then, who are evil, know how to give good gifts to your children, how much more will the heavenly Father give the Holy Spirit to those who ask Him?..."

(Lk 11: 13 HCSB)

The Holy Spirit

"I am sending the promise of My Father upon you;
but stay… until clothed with power from on high."
(Lk 24: 49)

Another Advocate – to be with you always

And I will ask the Father, and He will give you another Advocate to be with you always, the spirit of truth,… it remains with you, and will be in you."

(Jn. 14: 16 – 17 NABRE).

Walk by the Spirit

"…walk by the spirit and you will not carry out the desire of the flesh." (Gal 5: 16)

On the contrary, the works of the flesh are "sexual immorality, moral impurity, promiscuity, idolatry, sorcery, hatreds, strife, jealousy, outbursts of anger, selfish ambitions, dissensions, factions, envy, drunkenness, carousing, and anything similar."

"We must not become conceited, provoking one another, envying one another." (Gal 5: 16, 22-23, 19-21, 26)

For more on this theme, you will profit by reading: Eph. 5:9-10; 2Cor. 6:3-10;

1Tim. 4:12, 16; 2Pt. 1:5-7.

Different Gifts, One Giver, One Purpose

"For as the body is one and has many parts … so we are 'the body of Christ, and individual members of it.'" (1 Cor. 12:12, 27 HCSB)

"Now there are different gifts, but the same spirit. There are different ministries, but the same Lord. And there are different activities, but the same God activates each gift in each person." (1Cor. 12:4-6).

Apostles, prophets – healers, helpers, managers and speakers in tongues.

"… God has put the body together,… **so that there would be no division in the body**, but that the members would have the same concern for each other. So if one member suffers, all the members suffer with it; if one member is honoured, all the members rejoice with it." (1Cor. 12:24-26).

For the full message read 1Cor. 12:1-30.

At the approach of the end time –

"After this

I will pour out My Spirit on all humanity; then your sons and your daughters will prophesy, your old men will have dreams, and your young men will see visions.

I will even pour out My Spirit on the male and female slaves in those days."

(Joel 2:28-29) (Act 2-17)

Test the spirits

"Dear friends, do not believe every spirit, but test the spirits to determine if they are from God, because many false prophets have gone out into the world.

: 2 This is how you know the Spirit of God: Every spirit who confesses that Jesus Christ has come in the flesh is from God.

: 3 But every spirit who does not confess Jesus, is not from God. This is the spirit of the antichrist;…"

"We are from God. Anyone who knows God listens to us; anyone who is not from God does not listen to us. From this we know the Spirit of truth and the spirit of deception." (1 Jn 4: 1-3, 6)

The testimony of three

"Jesus Christ – He is the One who came by water and blood,… And the Spirit is the One who testifies, because the Spirit is the truth. For there are three that testify: the Spirit, the water and the blood – and these three are in agreement."

(1 Jn. 5:6-8)

The Spirit in Man

"Thus says God, the Lord,
Who created the heavens and stretched them out,
Who spread out the earth and its produce,
Who gives breath to its people
and spirit to those who walk on it" (Isa. 42: 5 NABRE)

The Spirit is of Power, not of fear!

"For God has not given us a spirit of fearfulness, but one of power, love, and sound judgement." (2 Tim. 1: 7 HCSB).

The Holy Spirit

"Is the down payment of our inheritance for the redemption of the possession to the praise of His glory." (Eph. 1:14 HCSB)

God shows no favouritism; He pours the Holy Spirit on the person who fears Him and does righteousness including gentiles. (Acts 10: 34 – 35; 44 – 45 HCSB).

The Spirit is power of God

"…I am sending the promise of My Father upon you; but stay in the city until you are clothed with power from on high. (Lk 24:49 NABRE).

The Fruits of the Spirit

The fruit of the Spirit is love, joy, peace, patience, kindness, generosity, faithfulness, gentleness, self-control.

"We must not become conceited, provoking one another, envying one another."

(Gal. 5:22-23, 26)

The thoughts of God

"… Similarly, no one knows what pertains to God except the Spirit of God."
(1 Cor. 2: 11 NABRE)

The Spirit and your call

"…from the beginning God has chosen you for salvation through sanctification by the Spirit and through belief in the truth." (2 Thes. 2: 13 HCSB)

TEST

There is spirit of truth and there is spirit of deception. (1 Jn. 4: 1-3)

The Holy Spirit testified (truthfully) that Jesus is the Son of God (1 Jn. 5: 6)

The Counsellor or Advocate or Helper

"This is the Spirit of truth. The world is unable to receive Him because it doesn't see Him or know Him… He remains with you and will be in you." (Jn. 14: 17).

The Ministry of the Holy Spirit

 i. "The Helper, the Holy Spirit, whom the Father will send in My name, will teach you everything and make you remember all that I have told you." (Jn. 14: 26 GNBDK)

 ii. "…And when He has come, He will convict the world of sin, and of righteousness, and of judgement". (Jn. 16: 8 NKJV)

Another Version put it this way,

"And when He comes, He would prove the world wrong about sin and righteousness and judgement." (Jn. 16: 8 NRSV –CI).

For more on this topic read (Jn 16: 9-11, 13-15)

Another Helper – The Spirit of Truth

"If you love Me, you will obey My commandments
I will ask the Father, and He will give you another Helper, who will stay with you forever; He is the Spirit who reveals the truth about God…"
(Jn. 14: 15 – 17; 15 GNBDK)

Foreboding

"And now I am on my way to Jerusalem, bound in My Spirit, not knowing what I will encounter there, except that in town after town the Holy Spirit testifies to me that chains and afflictions are waiting for me."

"And now I know that none of you will ever see my face again – …."

Paul's farewell address to Ephesus elders (Acts 20: 22-23 HCSB)

Speaking in tongues

i. Strive for love and empowerment to proclaim God's message (prophesy).

"It is love, then, that you should strive for. Set your hearts on spiritual gifts, especially the gift of proclaiming God's message."

ii. "Those who speak in strange tongues do not speak to others but to God, because no one understands them. They are speaking secret truths by the power of the Spirit." (1 Cor. 14: 1, 3 GNBDK)

iii. "Those who speak in strange tongues help only themselves,…" "unless there is someone present who can explain what is said,… (1Cor. 14:4, 5 GNBDK)

iv. "… how will anyone understand what you are talking about if your message is given in strange tongues… Your words will varnish in the air!"

"The person who speaks in strange tongues, then, must pray for the gift to explain what is said…" (1Cor. 14:9, 13 GNBDK)

i.   "… If I pray in this way, my spirit prays indeed; but my mind has no part in it."

"…I will (rather) pray with my spirit, but… also with my mind;… sing with my spirit but… also with my mind." (1 Cor. 14: 14 – 15 GNBDK)

"In scripture it was written: '… but even then My people will not listen to Me'. So then,… speaking in strange tongues is proof for unbelievers, while …proclaiming God's message is proof for believers,…" "But if everyone is proclaiming God's message… unbelievers or ordinary people… will be convinced of their sin by what they hear, … bow down and worship God, confessing, 'Truly, God is here among you!'"(1 Cor. 14: 21-22, 24-25 GNBDK)

Miraculous healings by Jesus' Disciples

"… Many wonders and signs were being performed through the Apostles."

(Acts 1:43; 5:12)

Here are some:

i. MAN BORN CRIPPLED full texts: Acts 3: 1 – 10

Peter and John went to the Temple complex at three p.m. to pray. A man lame from birth, who begs for alms at the temple gate, called, 'Beautiful', saw them and begged for help.

"Silver or gold I have not; what I have I give you: In the name of Jesus, the Nazarene, get up and walk!" Peter said.

"…at once his feet and ankles became strong. So he jumped up, stood and started to walk,… entered the Temple… walking, leaping, and praising God."

(Acts 3:6-8 HCSB)

i. THE HOLY SPIRIT AT THE HOME OF UNCIRCUMCISED CORNELIUS

"Cornelius said, '…three days ago… I was praying in my house at three o'clock in the afternoon.

Suddenly, a man dressed in shinning clothes stood in front of me and said, "Cornelius! … Send someone to Joppa for a man whose full name is Simon Peter. He is a guest in the home of Simon, the tanner of leather who lives by the sea.'"

"While Peter was still speaking, the Holy Spirit came down on all who were listening to his message.'"… they heard them speaking in strange tongues and praising God's greatness." (Acts 10: 30-32, 44, 46. GNBDK)

iii. A SORCERER OPPOSED THE MESSAGE

Paul, Barnabas and John Mark came to Paphos. They came across a sorcerer, a Jewish false prophet named Bar-Jesus. He was with the Pro consul, Sergius Paulus... "But Elymas the sorcerer… opposed them and tried to turn the Proconsul away from the faith."

"… Paul ….said … 'Now look! The Lord's hand is against you. You are going to be blind … for a time'. Suddenly…. he went around seeking someone to lead him by the hand." (Acts 13: 6-9)

The Holy Spirit at Jesus Baptism

"And the Holy Spirit descended on Him in a physical appearance like a dove.

And a voice came from heaven:
You are My beloved Son
I take delight in You!" (Lk. 3: 22 HCSB)

My Servant, My Chosen One: My Spirit upon Him

"Here is My Servant whom I uphold.
My Chosen One with whom I am pleased.

Upon Him I have put My Spirit
He shall bring forth justice to the nations." (Isa. 42: 1 NABRE)

Streams of Living Water

- "If anyone is thirsty, he should come to Me and drink! The one who believes in Me, as the scripture has said will have streams of living water flow from deep within him." "He said this about the Spirit…" (Jn. 7: 38, 39 HCSB).
- "With joy you will draw water from the fountain of salvation." (Isa. 12: 3)
- "On that day living water will flow out of Jerusalem…"
- On that day Yahweh will become King over all the earth – Yahweh alone and His name alone." (Zech. 4: 8, 9 HCSB)

ADDITIONAL RESOURCES

HOLY SPIRIT BAPTISM

"Paul said,

'John baptized with a baptism of repentance,

telling the people that they should

believe in the One who would come

after him, that is, in Jesus."

"When they heard this, they were baptized

in the name of the Lord Jesus.

And when Paul had laid his hands on them,

the Holy Spirit came on them,

and they began to speak in other languages

and to prophesy."

Now there were about 12 men in all

(Acts 19: 4-7 HCSB)

The Messiah gave gifts

"For the training of the saints in the work of ministry, to build up the body of Christ

until we all reach unity in the faith and in the knowledge of God's Son…"

(Eph 4: 12-13 HCSB)

The Counsellor's Ministry – Witnessing:

"When the Counsellor comes the One I will send to you from the Father – the Spirit of Truth who proceeds from the Father – He will testify about Me." (Jn 15: 26 HCSB)

"When He comes, He will *convict* the world about sin, righteousness and judgement." (Jn 16: 8)

Convict: "prove to the word that they are wrong" (GNBDK)

Judgement: "condemnation" (NABRE)

"About sin, because they do not believe in Me;

About righteousness, because I am going to the Father and, you will no longer see Me; and about judgement, because the ruler of this world has been judged" (Jn 16: 9-11 HCSB)

"Now is the time of judgement on this world; now the ruler of this world will be driven out." (Jn 12: 31)

See also (Rev: 9, 11)
Exhortation, meditation and reflection

Spirit of Light; spirit of darkness

God gave His Word incarnated in the Blessed Virgin Mary to go and experience the world, cleave the darkness of falsehood, revealing the truth as darkness gives way before light. He is to sanctify the world with His own precious blood (thus sparing us of condemnation) and reconciling us back to the Father, the fountain of the Divinity. The Holy Spirit assists in this mission.

"But the counsellor, the Holy Spirit – the Father will send Him in My name – will teach you all things and remind you of everything I have told you."

(Jn. 14: 26).

"But you will receive power when the Holy Spirit has come on you, and you will be My witnesses in Jerusalem, in all Judea and Samaria, and to the end of the earth. (Acts 1:8).

What the Holy Spirit does – Don Schwager[1]

"The Holy Spirit makes faith come alive within us"

"Those who are humble and hungry for God receive His Spirit"

"The Holy Spirit is God's gift to us to enable us to know and experience the indwelling presence of God and the power of His Kingdom"

"The Holy Spirit is the way in which God reigns within each of us."

The Ministry of the Holy Spirit

Eldad and Medad: selected and appointed; approved and anointed.

70 elders were selected and appointed to assist Moses.

Two, Eldad and Medad, failed to attend the Tent of Meeting. The elders who attended became prophets. At the same time, these two also began prophesying, even in the camp! (Num 11: 26-30)

What does that tell us? That God loves to work in collaboration with man? That He is cognizant of due protocol, understanding our weaknesses?

These seem to be the understanding of the early fathers of our faith when they selected a replacement for fallen Apostle Judas Iscariot and the tradition persists by electing successors to the Rock, Simon Peter; appointing priests and bishops by the invocation of the Holy Spirit and laying of hands by these leaders.

1: Don Schwager, Aug.15, 2018. Website: DailyScripture:Servants of The Word.org © 2018.

Consider also all the 70 or 72 that Jesus sent out on the second missionary campaign; they all performed the function of prophets in their respective missions.

"THE HOLY SPIRIT"

"The spirit is the source of holiness, a spiritual light, and He offers His own light to every mind

to help it in its search for truth… the power of the Spirit fills the whole universe, but He gives himself only to those who are worthy, acting in each according to the measure of his faith."

"Simple in Himself, the Spirit is manifold in His mighty works. The whole of His being is present everywhere. Though shared in by many, He remains unchanged; His self-giving is no loss to Himself. Like the sunshine, which permeates all the atmosphere, spreading over land and sea, and yet is enjoyed by each person as though it were for him alone, so the Spirit pours forth His grace in full measure, sufficient for all, and yet is present as though exclusively to everyone who can receive Him. To all creatures that share in Him He gives a delight limited only by their own nature, not by His ability to give."

"The Spirit raises our hearts to heaven, guides the steps of the weak, and brings to perfection those who are making progress. He enlightens those who have been cleansed from every stain of sins and makes them spiritual by communion with Himself.

As clean, transparent substances become very bright when sunlight falls on them and shine with a new radiance, so also souls in whom the Spirit shines become spiritual themselves and a source of grace for others.

From the Spirit comes fore-knowledge of the future, understanding of the mysteries of faith, insight into the hidden meaning of scripture and other special gifts. Through the Spirit we become citizens of heaven, we enter into eternal happiness, and abide in God. Through the Spirit we acquire likeness to God."

Above is a perspective of the Holy Spirit by St Basil, the great, bishop.

http://www.CatholicSaints|Saint/Basil.com

CHAPTER 5

Mary, Joseph and Jesus' Disciples

ARE YOU CALLED?
"IF you love Me, you will keep My commandments." (Jn 14: 15)
"This is how all will know that you are My disciples,
if you have love for one another." (Jn 13: 35 NABRE)
We are Jesus' brothers and sisters IF
we do the will of God – (Lk 8: 21)
'On that day many will say to Me,
'Lord, Lord! Didn't we prophesy in Your name,
drive out demons in Your name, and do many
miracles in Your name?"
The Lord will respond,
'I never knew you; depart from Me,
you evildoers.' (Matt 7: 22-23)
"Not everyone… will enter the kingdom of heaven, but only the
one who does the will of My Father…" (Matt 7: 21)
FLEE!
"When they persecute you in one town
Flee to another." (Matt 10: 23 NABRE)
They jeered even at Jesus!
"The Pharisees, who were lovers of money,
were listening to all these things and scoffing at Him." (Lk 16:
14 HCSB)
"…the Lord ordered that those who preach the gospel should
live by the gospel." (1 Cor 9: 14)
FELLOWSHIP
  ▪ Our fellowship is with God through His Son.
His anointing gives us knowledge; therefore,

OBEY Him and walk as He walked (1 Jn 1: 3, 6-7, 27; 2: 4-6; 3: 24)

- Many invited, few chosen.

"For many are invited, but few are chosen." (Matt 22: 14)

The rich official Lk 18: 18-23, had the invitation extended to him, but…

Zacchaeus, the chief tax collector, was ready to answer the call, though no-one suspected it! (Lk 19: 1-10)

CHRISTIAN MINISTRY: "That repentance, for the forgiveness of sins would be preached in His name to all nations." (Lk 24: 47)

Jesus says: "IF you continue in My word, you really are My disciples.

You will know the truth, and the truth will set you free." (Jn 8: 31-32)

Authority to preach the gospel

"Go into the world and preach the gospel to the whole creation…."

(Mk 16: 15-16)

Worldliness – Be detached!

"Do not love the world or the things that belong to the world…" (1 Jn 2: 15-17)

Christian fellowship

Seeking justice from an unjust system?

"IF any of you has a legal dispute against another, do you dare go to court before the unrighteous, and not before the saints?

"I say this to your shame! Can it be that there is not one wise person among you who is able to arbitrate between his brothers?

"Instead, believer goes to court against believer, and that before unbelievers!

Therefore to have legal disputes against one another is already a moral failure for you. Why not rather put up with injustice? Why not rather be cheated?"

(1 Cor 6: 1, 5-7 HCSB)

For more, read 1 Cor 6: 1-11

Warning against presumption – 1 Cor 10: 1-13

"Therefore whoever thinks he is standing

secure should take care not to fall." (1 Cor 10: 12)

The Truth and freedom from Fear, anxiety, moral turpitude, etc.

"You will know the truth, and the truth will set you free" (Jn 8: 31)

CLING TO JESUS, the vine

Jesus says:

"I am the vine and My Father is the vine grower. He takes away every branch in Me that does not bear fruit, and everyone that does He prunes so that it bears more fruit. You are already pruned because of the word that I spoke to you. Remain in Me, as I remain in you. Just as a branch cannot bear fruit on its own unless it remains on the vine, so neither can you unless you remain in Me. I am the vine, you are the branches. Whoever remains in Me and I in him will bear much fruit, because without Me you can do nothing." (Jn 15: 1-5 NABRE)

Read the entire discuss, Jn 15: 16-17.

My flesh, … My blood (the communion)

"The one who eats My flesh and drinks My blood lives in Me, and I in him."

(Jn 6: 56)

Not everybody can bear this:

"This teaching is hard! Who can accept it?" (Jn 6: 60, 66 HCSB)

Eating the flesh and drinking the blood: The metaphor explained.

"As they were eating, He took the bread… gave it to them, and said, 'Take it; this is My body.'

Then He took a cup,… He gave it to them and so they all drank from it. He said to them,

'This is My blood… it is shed for many.'" (Mk 14: 22-24 HCSB)

"Your life should be free from the love of money.

Be satisfied with what you have, for He Himself has said, I will never leave you or forsake you." (Heb 13: 5)

Likewise read Evangelist Matthew's account of same in Matt 26: 26-28.

The word

"Do not hold back a word.

Perhaps they will listen and return – each

from his evil way of life." (Jer 26: 2, 3 HCSB)

"IF you remain in Me and My word remain in you,

ask… and it will be done for you." (Jn 15: 7 NABRE)

The one who has is given more

"…Because knowledge of the mysteries of the kingdom of heaven has been granted to you,…To anyone who has, more will be given and he will grow rich; from anyone who has not, even what he has will be taken away."

(Matt 13: 11-12 NABRE)

Service: the greatest.

"…the rulers of the Gentiles dominate them, and the men of high position exercise power over them. It must not be like that among you. On the contrary, whoever wants to become great among you must be your servant, and whoever wants to be first… must be your slave; just as the Son of Man did not come to be served, but to serve and …." (Matt 20: 25-28)

In the kingdom of God, it is SERVICE, not servitude.

1 Pt 5:5 "Be servants of each other."

Ministry of Reconciliation

Everything is from God, who reconciled us to Himself through Christ… That is, in Christ, God was reconciling the world to Himself, not counting their trespasses against them, and He has committed the message of reconciliation to us. Therefore… we plead on Christ behalf, "Be reconciled to God." He made the one who did not know sin to be sin for us, so that we might become the righteousness of God in Him."

(2 Cor 5: 18-21)

The pillar and foundation of the truth

"…God's household, which is the church of the living God, (is) the pillar and foundation of the truth"
(1 Tm 3: 15)

A vocation of service

"So if I, your Lord and Teacher, have washed your feet, you also ought to wash one another's feet. For I have given you an example that you also should do just as I have done for you." (Jn 13: 14-15)

Light and Darkness:

i.   Jesus: The Light of the World
"I am the light of the world. Anyone who follows Me will never walk in the darkness but will have
the light of life." (Jn 8: 12)

ii.   For this purpose, disciples of Jesus are to be the salt of the earth and the lamp of the world (Matt 5: 13-16)

iii. "This, then, is the judgement: the light has come into the world, and people loved darkness rather than the light because their deeds were evil. For everyone who practises wicked things hates the light and avoids it, so that his deeds may not be exposed. But anyone who lives by the truth comes to the light, so that his works may be shown to be accomplished by God." (Jn 3: 19-21)

How to resolve disputes between brothers

"If your brother sins against you, go and rebuke him in private. If he listens to you, you have won your brother. But if he won't listen, take one or two more with you so that… every fact may be established. If he pays no attention to them, tell the church…"

"I assure you: whatever you bind on earth is bound in heaven, and whatever you loose on earth is already loosed in heaven." (Matt 18: 15-18)

Be perfect!

This is how –

"IF you want to be perfect,... go, sell your belongings and give it to the poor, and YOU WILL HAVE TREASURE IN HEAVEN. Then come, FOLLOW ME."

(Matt 19: 21) (*Capitals mine)*

Read also Matt 5: 44-45.

Be mindful to practise what you preach

"They tie up heavy loads that are hard to carry and put them on people's shoulders, but they themselves aren't willing to lift a finger to move them."

(Matt 23: 4)

For more of the expectations from you as a disciple read Matt 23: 1-36

Do Nothing... but think the same way, have the same goal

"Fulfil My joy by thinking the same way, having the same love, sharing the same feelings, focusing on one goal. Do nothing out of rivalry or conceit, but in humility consider others as more important than yourselves. Everyone should look out not only for his own interests, but also for the interests of others."

(Phil 2: 2-4)

Bear Fruit

Parable of the Vine and the branches: you had better bear fruit and your grace will be abundant.

Parable of talents: use it else you lose it! You are going to account for what you do with it. (Matt 25: 14-30; Lk 19: 12-27)

Like Master, like servant

"Can the blind guide the blind?

Won't they both fall into a pit?

A disciple is not above his teacher, but everyone who is fully trained will be like his teacher." (Lk 6: 39-40 HCSB)

Temperance

"…When we are reviled, we bless; when we are persecuted, we endure it; when we are slandered, we respond graciously. Even now, we are like the world's garbage, like the dirt everyone scrapes off their sandals." (1 Cor 4: 11, 12 HCSB)

My Father's glory is shown by your bearing much fruit; And in this way you become My disciples.

If you obey My commands, you will remain in My love, just as I have obeyed My Father's commands and remain in His love…" (Jn 15: 8, 10 GNBDK)

The Promise
i. Eternal life

"I assure you: Anyone who hears My word and believes Him-who-sent-Me has eternal life and will not come under judgement…"

(Jn 5: 24, *special punctuation ours*)

ii. The Holy Spirit

"But the Counsellor, the Holy Spirit – the Father will send Him in My name – will teach you all
things and remind you of everything I have told you." (Jn 14: 26)

iii. Love Jesus.

"Jesus answered,
'If anyone loves Me, he will keep My word.
My Father will love him, and we will come to him and
make Our home with him.'" (Jn 14: 23)

The Investiture

Jesus declared,

iv. Greater works

"I assure you: The one who believes in Me will also do
the works that I do. And he will do even greater works than these,
because I am going to the Father." (Jn 14: 12)

v. Asking in My name

"whatever you ask in My name, I will do it so that
the Father may be glorified in the Son. If you ask Me
anything in My name, I will do it." (Jn 14: 13-14)
The 30 and the 50,000 pieces of silver
In Matt 27: 3, 5, the people (Jews) valued the Lord for 30 pieces
of silver, the amount at which they valued the truth. But in Ephesus,
the cost of falsehood and deception was valued at 50,000 silver
pieces:
"…many of those who had practised magic collected their books
and burned them in front of everyone. So they calculated their value
and found it to be 50,000 pieces of silver." (Acts 19; 19 HCSB)

The communion

"(Take), My body" "…My blood" This is the main menu of this
banquet of His love.
(Jn 10: 18)
Under the typology or appearance of bread and wine (Matt 26:
26, 28; 1 Cor 11: 29) This is an allusion to the sacrificial death of
Jesus, the Lamb of God.
(Jn 1: 29, 36)
Healing at Lystra
"In Lystra a man… lame from birth… Paul said… 'Stand
upright!…' And he jumped up and started to walk around." (Acts 14:
8-11)
"And a man's enemies will be
the members of his household." (Matt 10: 36 HCSB)
Peter's Deliverance from Prison

"On the night before Herod was to bring him out for execution, Peter, bound with two chains was sleeping between two soldiers…" suddenly an angel of the Lord appeared,… and said "Quick, get up!"

"Get dressed… and follow me" so he went out and followed, and he did not know that what took place… was real, but thought he was seeing a vision."

They passed the first and second guard posts, they came to the Iron Gate… which opened to them by itself. They went outside… and immediately the angel left him."

Then Peter… went to the house of Mary, the mother of John Mark where many had gathered and were praying." (Acts 12: 6-10, 11, 12)

"Herod searched and did not find him (Peter), he interrogated the guards and ordered their execution." (Acts 12: 19)

DISCIPLESHIP

- Membership of God's family

"So then, you are no longer strangers and sojourners, but you are fellow citizens with the holy ones and members of the household of God."

(Eph 2: 19)

- Be warned against presumptive prophesy

"But the prophet who dares to speak a message in My name that I have not commanded him to speak, or … - that prophet must die"

(Deut 18:20 HCSB)

Humility: Be not called 'rabbi'!

"But as for you, do not be called 'Rabbi'…"

"The greatest among you will be your servant."

"Whoever exalts himself will be humbled,

And whoever humbles himself will be exalted."

(Matt 23: 8, 11-12 HCSB)

The Great Commission:

Go, witness for Me!

- "Go into the whole world and proclaim the gospel to every creature.

Whoever believes and is baptized will be saved; whoever does not believe will be condemned…"

(Mk 16: 15-16 NABRE)

All nations

- "…All power in heaven and on earth has been given to Me.

Go, therefore, and make disciples of all nations, baptizing them…

teaching them to observe all that I have commanded you. And behold I am with you always until the end of the age." (Matt 28: 18-20 NABRE)

"Jesus answered, 'If anyone loves Me, He will keep My word. My Father will love him, and …make Our home with him. The one who doesn't love Me will not keep My words…'" (Jn 14: 23, 24)

Disciples are the salt and the light

"You are the salt of the earth. But if the salt should lose its taste,…it's no longer good for anything but to be thrown out and trampled on by men.

You are the light of the world. A city situated on a hill cannot be hidden.

…a lamp…gives light for all…in the same way, let your light shine before men,… see your good works and give glory to your Father in heaven." (Matt 5: 13-16 HCSB)

Cost of discipleship: renounce family, self and possessions

Lk 14: 25 Once great crowds were going along with Jesus – He turned and told HCSB them:

Lk 14: 26 … anyone following Me who does not hate his own father, mother, HCSB wife, and children – he cannot be My disciple!

Lk 14: 27 "Whoever does not bear his own cross and come after Me cannot HCSB be My disciple."

Lk 14: 33 "In the same way, none of you can be My disciple unless you give up GNBDK everything you have."

Divine Gifts

No one can have anything… (Jn 3: 27 GNBDK)

"John responded,

'No one can receive a single thing unless it's given to him from heaven.'"

(Jn 3: 27 HCSB)

Virgin Mary, the Blessed Mother of Jesus (Lk 1: 26-28, 42)

"The Word became flesh and took up residence among us…full of grace and truth." (Jn 1: 1, 4, 14)

Jesus:

The Word – 1

"What was from the beginning…concerning the word of life – …the eternal life that was with the Father and was revealed to us – …we also declare to you…" (1 Jn 1: 1, 2, 3)

Jesus:

The Word – 2

In the beginning was the Word,

and the Word was with God,

and the Word was God.

Life was in Him

and that life was the light of men. (Jn 1:1, 4 HCSB)

Jesus:

An angel reveals to some shepherds in Judea:

"Don't be afraid, for look, I proclaim to you good news of great joy… for all the people…Today a Saviour, who is Messiah the Lord, was born for you In the city of David." (Lk 2: 10-11)

Mary:

Righteous and devout Simeon's prophecy: "…My eyes have seen Your salvation.

A light for revelation to the gentiles and glory to Your people Israel.

Then Simon blessed them and told His mother Mary: ' … - and a sword will pierce your own soul – that the thoughts of many hearts may be revealed.'"

(Lk 2:30, 32, 34, 35 HCSB)

ADDITIONAL RESOURCES

5. Mary, Joseph and Jesus' Disciples

Whoever is not against us, is for us.

Matt 9: 38 "'John said… Teacher we saw a man who was driving out demons in Your name, and we told him to stop, because he doesn't belong to our group'"

Matt 9: 39 "'Do not try to stop him, …'"

Matt 9: 40 "'FOR WHOEVER IS NOT AGAINST US, IS FOR US'"

"Follow Me!"

Lk 5: 27 NABRE "…He (Jesus) went out and saw a tax collector named Levi sitting at the customs post.

He said to him, 'follow Me.'

Lk 5: 28 And leaving everything behind, he got up and followed Him."

The Holy Spirit

Acts 8: 18 "When Simon saw that the Holy Spirit was given through the laying on of the Apostle's hands, he offered them money"

Acts 8: 20 "But Peter told him, 'may your silver be destroyed with you, because you thought the gift of God could be obtained with money.'"

Christian Unity

Acts 2: 44-45 "All who believed were together and had all things in common; they would sell their property and possessions and divide them among ALL according to each one's need."

See also (Acts 4: 32; 34-35 NABRE)

Don't be cause to sin Mk 12: 38-40 "Beware of the scribes, who… go around in long robes, and who HCSB want greetings in the market places, the front seats in the synagogues, and the places of honour at banquets.

They devour widow's houses and say long prayers just for show.

These will receive harsher punishment."

Insulted for Christ?

1 Pt 4: 14 If you are insulted for the name of Christ, blessed are you!

Power to All Apostles

Matt 18: 18 "whatever you bind on earth (re. recalcitrant brother)... is bound in (NABRE) heaven..."

Serve Christ, clothed with Him

Gal 3: 27 Being Clothed with Christ – no Jews, infidels etc. YOU ARE ALL ONE IN CHRIST!

Jn 12: 21 "... if anyone serves Me, the Father will honour him."

Upon this rock I will build My church

Matt 16: 16 Peter: "You are the Messiah, the Son of the Living God"

Matt 16: 18 "You are Peter and upon this rock I will build My church and the gate of ..."

Matt 16: 19 "I will give you the keys to the kingdom of heaven, whatever you bind on earth shall be bound in heaven; and whatever you loose

on earth shall be loosed in heaven." (c/f Matt 18: 18)

(Comment: Jesus' church means the community that Jesus will gather with Peter as chief witness thereof) Read also Matt 16: 24-27: Condition for Discipleship: self-denial, bear own cross (NABRE)

Not thinking as God does?

Matt 16: 23 "...an obstacle... You are thinking not as God does but as human beings do."

The ELEVEN (i.e., without Judas Iscariot):

"...Peter, John, James, Andrew, Philip, Thomas, Bartholomew, Matthew, James son of Alphaeus, Simon the Zealot, and Judas the son of James"

(Acts 1: 13 HCSB)

"- the number of people who were together was about 120 - ..."

(Acts 1: 15 HCSB)

JESUS, MARY, JOSEPH (HOLY FAMILY)

Jesus

"Praise the Lord, the God of Israel, because He has visited and provided redemption for His people … a horn of salvation … in the house of His servant David" (Lk 1:68, 69) HCSB

"Because of our God's merciful compassion, the Dawn from on high will visit us: to shine on those who live in darkness … to guide our feet in the way of peace." (Lk 1:78, 79) HCSB

Devil tests Him, angels serve Him.

"Then the Devil left Him, and immediately angels came and began to serve Him." (Matt 4:11) HCSB

"Then an angel from heaven appeared to Him, strengthening Him."

(Lk 22:43) HCSB

Virgin Mother Mary

"… the angel Gabriel was sent from God … to a virgin betrothed to a man named Joseph, of the house of David, and the virgin's name was Mary."

(Lk 1:26-27) NABRE

"Rejoice …! The Lord is with you.

Do not be afraid, Mary, for you have found favour with God. … You will conceive and give birth to a son … Jesus. He will be great and … called the Son of the Most High, and … God will give Him the throne of his father David. He will reign … forever, and His kingdom will have no end." (Lk 1:28, 30, 31-33, HCSB)

"Elizabeth was filled with the Holy Spirit. Then she exclaimed … 'you are the most blessed of women, and your child will be blessed! How could this happen to me, that the mother of my Lord should come to me?'" (Lk 1:41-43) HCSB

(Mary responded): "…Surely from now on all generations will call me blessed, …" (Lk 1:48, HCSB)

The womb that bore Jesus

As Jesus was speaking to the crowd "a woman from the crowd raised her voice and said to Him,

'The womb that bore You and the one who nursed You are blessed!'

He said, 'Even more, those who hear the word of God and keep it are blessed.'" (Lk 11: 27-28 HCSB)

Mary

"…Elizabeth was filled with the Holy Spirit. Then she spoke out with a loud voice and said,

'Blessed are you among women, and blessed is the fruit of your womb!'" (Lk 1: 41, 42 NKJV)

Mary

then He said to the disciple, "Behold your mother!" (Jn 19:27 NKJV)

MARY – A SIGN

"To that Isaiah replied,

'Listen now, descendants of King David…

Well then, the Lord Himself will give you a sign:

a young woman who is pregnant will have a son

and will name Him 'Emmanuel'.'" (Isa 7: 13, 14 GNBDK)

Joseph, the husband of Mary (Lk 1: 26-27)

- "We found the One Moses wrote about in the Law (and so did the prophets): Jesus the Son of Joseph, from Nazareth!" (Jn 1: 45)

Genealogy:

- "Eliud fathered Eleazer, Eleazer fathered Matthan, Matthan fathered Jacob,

and Jacob fathered Joseph the husband of Mary, who gave birth to Jesus who is called the Messiah." (Matt 1: 15-16)

The angel in Joseph's dream said to him,

- "Joseph, Son of David, don't be afraid to take Mary as your wife, because what has been conceived in her is by the Holy Spirit. She will give birth to a Son, and you are to name Him Jesus…" (Matt 1: 20, 21)
- "When Joseph got up from sleeping, he did as the Lord's angel had commanded him. He married her." (Matt 1: 24)

The Caesar Augustus nativity registration

- "And Joseph went up from the town of Nazareth in Galilee, to Judea, to the city of David, which is called Bethlehem, because he was of the house and family line of David, to be registered along with Mary, who was engaged to him and was pregnant." (Lk 2: 4-5) To Egypt, Flee; Return!
- "…an angel of the Lord suddenly appeared to Joseph in a dream, saying, 'Get up! Take the child and His mother, flee to Egypt, and stay there until I tell you…'

So, he got up, took the child and His mother during the night, and escaped to Egypt."

- "After Herod died, an angel of the Lord suddenly appeared in a dream to Joseph in Egypt, saying, 'Get up! Take the child and His mother and go to the land of Israel, because those who sought the child's life are dead.' So, he got up, took the child and His mother, and entered the land of Israel."

"And being warned in a dream, he withdrew to the region of Galilee."
(Matt 2: 13-14; 19-21, 22)

Joseph

- "… when Joseph got up from sleeping, … he married her."
- "… flee to Egypt … So he got up … during the night, and escaped to Egypt."
- "So he got up took the child and his mother and entered … Israel." (Matt 1:24; 2:13, 14; 21 HCSB)

Parental anxieties over the missing child Jesus (Lk 2: 41-50)

Every year Joseph and Mary with the child Jesus, would travel to Jerusalem for the Passover festival.

The pilgrimage when Jesus was twelve years old was remarkable as "the boy Jesus stayed behind in Jerusalem, but His parents did not know it."

They returned to Jerusalem and for 3 days searched for Him. When they eventually found Him out, it was in the temple and this drama played out:

Jesus:

"Your father", "My Father"

Mary: "Son, why have you treated us like this? Your father and I have been anxiously searching for You."

Jesus: "Why were you searching for Me?

Didn't you know that I had to be in My Father's house?" (Lk 2:48-49 HCSB)

Intercession

"All the people witnessed the thunder and lightning, the sound of the trumpet, and the mountain surrounded by smoke …

'You speak to us, and we will listen', they said to Moses, 'but don't let God speak to us or we will die'.

Moses responded … 'God has come to test you, so that you will fear Him and will not sin.'"

(Exo 20:18, 19, 20) HCSB

"Who among you fears the Lord,

Listening to the voice of His Servant? Who among you walks in darkness; and has no light?

Let him trust in the name of Yahweh; let him lean on his God." (Isa 50:10) HCSB

The goal of our faith – discipleship

"(May) the God of our Lord Jesus Christ, the father of glory, … give you a spirit of wisdom and revelation resulting in knowledge of Him.

May the eyes of (your) hearts be enlightened, that you may know what is the hope that belongs to His call, what are the riches of glory in His inheritance … and what is the surpassing greatness of His power for us who believe, in accord with … His great might, … in Christ, … far above every principality, authority, power and dominion, and every name …" (Eph 1:17-21) NABRE

Call to evangelize – the promise:

"And I say to you, anyone who acknowledges Me before men, the Son of Man will also acknowledge him before the angels of God." (Lk 12:8) HCSB

Forgive sins, and heaven will forgive them!

Jesus endowed His disciples with power to forgive sins, saying. "Receive the Holy Spirit. If you forgive the sins of any, they are forgiven them; if you retain the sins of any, they are retained."
(Jn 20:22, 23) HCSB

God is our Father!

"See what love the father bestowed on us that we may be called, the children of God. Yet so we are. What we should be has not been revealed … we do know we shall be like Him."
Lk 14:11 HCSB Humility
"For everyone who exalts himself will be humbled, but the one who humbles himself will be exalted."

Desirous of wealth?

"But those who want to be rich fall into temptation, a trap, and many foolish and harmful desires, which plunge people into ruin and destruction.
For the love of money is a root of all kinds of evil, and by craving it, some have wandered away from the faith …" (1 Jn 6:9-10, HCSB)
Our circumcision/Christian initiation "You were also circumcised in Him with a circumcision not done with hands, … in the circumcision of the messiah." (Col 2:11, HCSB)
Even Moses had admonished the people:
"Therefore, circumcise your hearts and don't be stiff-necked any longer"
(Deut 10:16 HCSB)

God's People

Coming, coming … the Lord has come!

"Daughter Zion, shout for joy and be glad, for I am coming to dwell among you" – this is the Lord's declaration

"Many nations will join themselves to the Lord on that day and become My people. I will dwell among you, and you will know that the Lord of Hosts has sent Me to you.

Let all people be silent before the Lord, for He is coming from His holy dwelling." (Zec 2:10-11, 13, HCSB) (c/fZec 2:14-15, 17 NABRE)

The prophet's disciple, Elisha.

Note that Elijah did not specifically allow Elisha to go and bid good bye to his parents (1 Kgs 19:19-21)

Jesus command to all disciples (i.e., Christians): "Love!"

My Command: "Love one another ..." Jesus told His disciples.

"...Remain in My love. If you keep My commands you will remain in my love, ...

This is my command: Love one another as I have loved you."

Jesus Friends: "You are My friends if you do what I command you."

"This is what I command you: love one another." (Jn 15: 9-10, 12, 14, 17, HCSB)

The Kingdom Secrets

"...The secrets of the kingdom of heaven have been given for you to know, but it has not been given to them (non-disciples)" (Matt 13:10, HCSB)

Jesus' Ministry, our obligation.

"I must proclaim the good news of the kingdom of God, because for this purpose I have been sent." (Lk 4:43, lect.)

Disciples' reward – heaven is the goal!

"Nevertheless, ... but rejoice because your names are written in heaven."
(Lk 10:20, NABRE)
(See also Exo 32:32)
Listening to Jesus
"Whoever listens to you, listens to Me.
Whoever receives you receives Me and whoever receives Me, receives the One who sent Me."
(Lk 10:16; Matt 10:40, NABRE)
Mary's Precept
"Do whatever He (Jesus) tells you to do!" (Jn 2:5)

Saul, persecutor of Christians becomes a Christ's Witness! (For full insight read Acts 22: 3-16; 9:1-22, 28)

"I answered, 'Who are You, Lord?' He said to me, "I am Jesus the Nazarene ..."

"Someone named Ananias, a devout man ... having a good reputation with all the Jews residing there, came and stood by me and said, 'Brother Saul, regain your sight.' 'For you will be a witness for Him to all people ... be baptized, and wash away your sins by calling on His name.'"

"The following night, the Lord stood by him (Saul) and said, 'Have courage! For as you have testified about Me in Jerusalem, so you must also testify in Rome,'" (Acts 22:8, 12-13, 15-16; 23:11, HCSB)

The Church

"... God's household, which is the church of the living God, the pillar and foundation of the truth" (1 Tm 3:15, HCSB)
We Are God's Children

"We are God's children now, and what we will be has not yet been revealed. We know that when He appears, we will be like Him, because we will see Him…"

(1 Jn 3:2)

The Church (The New Jerusalem)

Then one of the seven angels spoke to me:

Rev 21:9 'Come, I will show you the bride, the wife of the Lamb.' He carried me away in the Spirit … and showed me the holy city, Jerusalem, coming down out of heaven from God, arrayed with God's glory".

: 12 The city had a massive high wall with 12 gates … the names of the 12 tribes of Israel's sons were inscribed on the gates."

: 14 "The city wall had 12 foundations, and the 12 names of the Lamb's 12 apostles were on the foundations …"

: 18 "The building material of its wall was jasper and the city was pure gold …"

: 19 "The foundations of the city wall were adorned with every kind of precious stone …"

: 22 "I did not see a sanctuary in it, because the Lord God the Almighty and the Lamb are its sanctuary."

: 23 The city does not need the sun or the moon to shine on it, because God's glory illuminates it, and its lamp is the Lamb."

: 27 Nothing profane will ever enter it: no one who does what is vile or false, but only those written in the Lamb's book of life."

22:1 "Then he showed me the river of living water … The tree of life was on both sides of the river … and there will no longer be any curse … and people .., will reign forever and ever." (Rev 21: 9-27; 22:1-5, HCSB)

Ungodly people barred from entry into the New Jerusalem

"… Worship God." Look! I am coming quickly, and My reward is with Me to repay each person according to what he has done. I am the Alpha and the Omega, the First and the Last, the Beginning and the End."

"Blessed are those who ... may have the right to ... enter the city ... Outside are the dogs, the sorcerers, the sexually immoral, the murderers, the idolaters and everyone who loves and practices lying."

(Rev. 22:9, 12-15, HCSB)

Exhortations, meditation and reflection.

MEDITATION: **Call to be God's people** – total submission to God

When we obey Christ, always and everywhere we seem to give up something very precious to us – our self-will!

In reality, we have given up nothing at all! We have only exchanged something of little or no merit for something of great value – our unrighteousness for the righteousness of God; our foolishness for the knowledge and wisdom that created the universe and made it to endure. We are certainly the better off for it. (Jesus is the refulgence of God's glory, Lk 14:28)

Discipleship reward: A hundred fold (Matt 19:29)

Those parting (from following Him) with what are most dear to them "will receive a hundred fold ... and eternal life."

Discipleship: Your Christian Identity

Your Christian initiation begins usually with the baptism of water for the renunciation of sins. It is usually preceded with catechesis – a process by which the candidate is informed about the significance of the process he is about to undergo.

Usually, after some further time had elapsed, the new convert receives the Holy Spirit baptism.

"We haven't even heard that there is a Holy Spirit." (Acts 19:2, HCSB)

With this the convert is a mature member of the body of Christ. But this does not mean that he is perfect.

"Be perfect as Your Father in heaven is perfect." (Matt 5:48)

Perfection comes through persistent practice of the faith being handed down through participation with others, studying of the scriptures and living the life:

"Therefore, as you have received Christ Jesus the Lord, walk in Him, rooted and built up in Him and established in the faith, just as you were taught, overflowing with gratitude." (Col 2:7 HCSB)

Exhortations, meditation and reflection.

Read also what Paul had to say further on this topic in Colossians chapter 3, especially Col 3:5-9; 12-16. This is the spiritual circumcision to which Christ has called us.

All these processes are geared toward one purpose – to make the converts disciples of the Lord Jesus.

Do you know, or can you imagine, what it is like to be a member of the household of God? Some may think this is simply preposterous; not a few may think it is blasphemous or outright contemptuous of God! But wait; here is – an invitation (to be a member of the household of God, the Most High):

"Then His mother and brothers came to Him, but they could not meet with Him because of the crowd. He was told, 'Your mother and Your brothers are standing outside, wanting to see you.' But He replied to them, 'My mother and My brothers are those who hear and do the word of God.'"

(Lk 8:19-21, HCSB)

What an exciting invitation to be members of the household of God by simply listening to and doing the word of God! The invitation is authentic, it comes from Jesus Christ, the Son of God

Compare Rev 12:17; Lk 11:28

"Even more, those who hear the word of God and keep it are blessed!"

"So then you are no longer strangers and sojourners, but you are fellow citizens with the holy ones and members of the household of God." (Eph 2:19)

JUSTIFICATION: sons of Abraham, sons of God!

Comments

I. "... Scripture makes no exceptions ... sin is master everywhere. In this way the promises (to Abraham and his descendants) ... can only be given to those who have this faith (in Jesus Christ).

"Merely by belonging to Christ (i.e., being baptized in Christ) you are the posterity of Abraham, the heirs he was promised."

Exhortations, meditation and reflection.

"The proof that you are (adopted) sons is that God has sent the Spirit of the Son, into our hearts: the spirit that cries, 'Abba, Father,' and it is this that makes you a son, ... and if God has made you son, then He has made you heir."

II. "The person who puts to death by the Spirit the deeds of our sinful nature will live, says the Apostle (Paul). This is not surprising since one who has the Spirit of God becomes a child of God ... so much so that the Holy Spirit bears witness to our Spirit that we are sons of God."

(Gal 3:15-4:7)

Idolatry: relationship (or possession) above God

"What do the twin parables of the tower builder and a ruler on a war campaign have in common (Lk 14: 28-32)? Both the tower builder and the ruler risked serious loss if they did not carefully plan ahead to make sure they could finish what they had begun."

"Paul, the Apostle reminds us, 'we are not our own. We were bought with a price' (1 Cor 6:19, 20). We were once slaves to sin... but we have now been purchased with the precious blood of Jesus Christ... so we could enter His kingdom of light and truth."

"To place any relationship or any possession above God is a form of idolatry – worshipping the creature in place of the creator..."Don Schwager

Lk 10: 27 Disciples must love God with all our hearts, minds, soul and strength.

Call to Special Ministries – Have you discerned your call?

Moses was to liberate the Israelites from enslavement and cruel labour in Egypt.

Jonah was sent to the Ninevites to liberate them from oppressive sin;

Cyrus to re-build Zion and its temple; Jehu to be king; Elisha to be prophet.

(1 Kgs 19: 16)

Gideon was sent to break the yoke of the Philistines' oppression;

St Patrick, to evangelize Ireland; St Martin de Porres, Mother Theresa of Calcutta, to bring succour to the hopeless and helpless in society; nurse Mary Slezzor – for Christian enlightenment in Calabar, Nigeria.

So you, too, must use your God-given resources, time, talent and treasure to address a Christian need that the Lord has inspired you to do.

"Based on the gift each one has received, use it to serve others as good managers of the varied grace of God." (1 Pt 4: 10)

Exhortations, meditation and reflection.

"We know that all things work together for the good of those who love God: those who are called according to His purpose." (Rom 8: 28)

A majority of the prophets are called for just one purpose – one mission: Elisha, to complete the work of Elijah; John the Baptist, to prepare the way for the Christ, and give witness to Him. What about you, have you discerned your call?

The Law:

Observe, the law and the prophets (Matt 7: 12) but besides, 'be perfect!'

Be Perfect!

"Be perfect, therefore, as Your heavenly Father is perfect." (Matt 5: 48)

Here is the perspective of St John of the Cross on this: 1 St John of the Cross – 1542 – 1591; Carmelite order

"IF you do not learn to deny yourself you can make no

progress in perfection. In detachment, the spirit finds quiet
and repose for coveting nothing.

Nothing wearies it by elation and nothing oppresses

it by dejection, because it stands in the center of its own
humility.

Live in the world as if only God and your soul were in it; then,
your heart will never be made captive by any earthly thing."

1.   Who is the greatest?

The disciples approached Jesus and asked, 'Who is the greatest
in the kingdom of heaven?'

For all so concerned, hear the Lord's response: be "converted
and become like children" if you would enter at all.

"Therefore, whoever humbles himself like this child… is the
greatest in the kingdom of heaven."

(Matt 18: 1-5)

1 St John of the Cross – 1542 – 1591; Carmelite order

Exhortations, meditation and reflection.

2.The First, the last?

Remember: In the parable of the labourers for the vineyard, they
were hired at, and worked for various hours. It pleased the master to
pay each of them the same amount – the usual daily wage.

(Matt 20: 1-15, 16)

No disciple is above his teacher,

No slave above his master.

It is enough for the disciple

that he become like his teacher,

for the slave that he become like his master… (Matt 10; 24, 25
NABRE)

Love of money

Money is good and necessary, but God is the Great Provider. He
knows what we need; He opens His hand and supplies all creatures
what they need.

You can't serve two masters – mammon and God. (Lk 16: 13)

Love of money is the root of all evil (1 Tm 6:10)

FREE!

"You have received free of charge; give free of charge.

…For the worker is worthy of his food." (Matt 10: 8, 10)

You will be hypocritical like the Pharisees, if you make money your god; for they, too, are misled by their love of money (Lk 16: 14) and position.

In the parable of the ten gold coins (Lk 19: 11-22, 23-26) – the stewards were empowered 'to each according to ability.'

Showing that our availability is more important than our ability. The Lord does not call the qualified but qualifies the called.

Meditation: Who is a disciple of the Lord Jesus?

All Christians are disciples each to the extent he or she keeps faith with the commandments of the Lord.

"By their fruits you shall know them" (Matt 7: 16, 20)

Exhortations, meditation and reflection.

Discipleship – a vocation.

Jesus preached the word at great personal sacrifice; large crowds converge on Him all the time and He never turned them away; rather, He would teach them. He and His disciples hardly had a private time. "They did not even have time to eat" (Mk 6: 31)

Thus is the service-oriented vocation of Christianity as exemplified by the Lord, Himself.

But it goes beyond belief or philosophy; it is a way of life – "the kingdom of heaven."

ORTHODOXY: Are you sure that you are standing right?

How are you sure you have not been swindled into false beliefs?

From earliest days – both Paul and the other Apostles – put down this rule of thumb: Any teaching different from those of the Apostles and others who have not gone away from them, is false and are to be avoided. From this grew the Apostolic Tradition.

The Lord has an inner caucus in Peter, James and John to whom many mysteries were exclusively revealed.

Finally the Lord established their collective leadership responsibility when He commissioned them:

"All authority has been given to Me in heaven and on earth. Go, therefore, and make disciples of all nations,…" (Matt 28: 18-20)

Before then, Peter's position was re-entrenched as the leader of the disciples

(Jn 21: 15-17)

For more see chapter 19, entitled "Be One"

To God be the glory:

"So whether you eat or drink or whatever… DO EVERYTHING FOR THE GLORY OF GOD." (1 Cor 10: 31 NABRE)

EXTRAORDINARY POWER

As a Christian or disciple of our Lord Jesus Christ, many are endowed with extraordinary gifts (for the ministry) – love, patience, piety, prophecy, healing, preaching and many others. How beautiful there gifts are when placed at the benefit of the body of Christ, and the entire society in which we live!

Exhortations, meditation and reflection.

If you do not see yourself as stewards for these gifts one could easily fall by the wayside and become arrogant. Learn from a master:

"Now we have this treasure in clay jars, so that this extraordinary power may be from God and not from us." (2 Cor 4: 7)

"God gave, that we may give."[2]

Cost of discipleship: Leave all!

"….first seat down and calculate the cost." (Lk 14: 28, 31)

But Lord, Who knows the future, other than the Lord God?

How could Moses, a fugitive, have accurately calculated what doing the work of God would entail compared with going blindfold into the future as shepherd of the flock of his father-in-law?

When Elisha received Elijah's mantle unexpectedly, how could he have compared his new calling with what he was then doing? "Leaving certainty for uncertainty," as they say?

Anybody who receives the call, should only consider the crown (i.e. the joy and fulfilment that we are serving God!) and never hesitate to make all he has available for the assignment plus prayer. Yes, because God empowers the called; those called must be prayerful. The statement of our Lord in Lk 14: 28 is to dampen the enthusiasm of the many, the throng who want the crown but shun the cross.

Which fun seeker or pleasure hunter would not be dismayed if called to be a 'Jesus', seeing the utterly self-less life the Lord lived? Or similar self-less life lived by Apostle Paul after his call? Like Simon and his brother Andrew, like James and his brother John, who left all – if you receive the call today, leave everything else and embrace it.

Know this, however, to succeed you will need to give up all other interests – family, friends, business, titles, etc.

May we not be possessed by our possessions. Amen.

Possessions

"…every one of you who does not renounce
all his possessions cannot be My disciple." (Lk 14: 33 NABRE)
2: Pope Benedict XVI – Daily meditations.
Exhortations, meditation and reflection.
Can you say with Peter,
'Look, we have left what we had
and followed You.'? (Lk 18: 28)
Discipleship entails nothing less.
He called Levi at his duty post, he left everything instantly and followed Him.
(Mk 2: 14)
Zacchaeus, the chief tax collector left all. (Lk 19: 2, 6, 8)
Reflect also on the two parables in Matt 13: 44-45: the prize – the kingdom of heaven – is a hidden treasure, a priceless pearl.

Resilience:

Like the guy constructing a tower or the beleaguered king with a force of 10,000 men confronting another power with 20,000 men each has to be sure his resources are adequate to the need. (Lk 14: 28-32) Thus balance what you seek to gain, the kingdom of heaven, with the cost of striving for it. (Detachment)

Purity – A requisite for discipleship.

"IF you repent, so that I restore you, in My presence you shall stand;

IF you bring forth the precious without the vile,

You shall be My mouthpiece." (Jer 15: 19 Lect)

"Can two walk together without

agreeing to meet?" (Amos 3: 3)

A Disciple Devoid of Piety?

You are a disciple of a religious founder like Moses, Jesus, Mohammed?

Or even of the founder of your local fellowship centre / 'church'?

Good! You give obeisance to this founder, but are you familiar with any deity to whom you give reverence and obedience?

Quite a number of people give adulation to this founder or the priest representing him whom they see and pay scant attention to the deity which is the object of the religion, of whom they rarely or never see.

Exhortations, meditation and reflection.

"The priests and prophets said to the princes and to all the people, 'this man deserves death; he has prophesied against this city…'" (Jer 26: 11 Lect)

The speakers are priests and prophets, the people closest to God whom you would expect to know the things of God better than the lay faithful. They are the ones orchestrating persecution of Jeremiah the Lord's prophet!… What an irony?

"That REPENTANCE for the FORGIVENESS of sins would be preached in His name to all the nations." (Lk 24: 47)

Discipleship Reward

"...'who, then, is the faithful and prudent steward whom the master will put in charge of His servants to distribute food allowance at the proper time? Blessed is that servant whom his master on arrival finds doing so.'" (Lk 12: 42-43)

"YOU are My witnesses...

and My servant whom I have chosen, so that you

may know and believe Me... that I am He.

No god was formed before Me

and there will be none after Me.

I, I Am Yahweh, and there is no other Saviour but Me." (Isa 43: 10-11 HCSB)

Sift and Sideline

"But now I am writing to you not to associate with anyone who claims to be a believer

who is sexually immoral or greedy, an idolater or verbally abusive, a drunkard or a swindler. Do not even eat with such a person."

"...put away the evil person from among yourselves" (1 Cor 5: 11, 13)

In the same context many religious people are so punctilious in the observance of the rites and rules of their faith but they hardly give a thought to the demands of the deity. Jesus chided the Pharisees and Sadducees for several of such practices. In our day, many religious people actually worship their founder, and feel that doing so they have satisfied all obligations! There is no fear of God in them! Such people are themselves – irascible, violent, greedy, arrogant, discriminating, self-centered, lying, etc.

Exhortations, meditation and reflection.

Outside the fellowship centre

Do you reason that different gods created different folks? It may, of course, massage your ego to think that your god is bigger and stronger than their gods; or that he fights for you against all others!

That overlooks the majestic beauty and coordination we find on earth and in the universe – implying a oneness in authority.

Personality worship automatically leads to discrimination, persecution, religious fanaticism and religious killing and killing for religion. Because the worshipper believes only in his religious founder/ leader but ignores the true God who created all of us and everything.

Love is the most poignant attribute of the sovereign God. He is the God of all – a righteous God who, wants mankind to treat each other with kindness. And whoever does what is right, is righteous. God loves the righteous; but hates wickedness, malice and all evils.

Thus, there are two families – the righteous and the ungodly. God's love has no leaning toward flesh and blood or to cult or clan. You can be assured that God loves you, if you are truly righteous.

First Missionary Commission: The Apostles

Summoning His 12 disciples, Jesus gave them authority over unclean spirits to drive them out, and to heal every disease and sickness. These are names of the 12 Apostles:

Simon Peter; his brother Andrew, James and his brother John, both sons of Zabedee Philip and Bartholomew; Thomas, Matthew, the tax collector, James, the son of Alphaeus, Thaddaeus, Simon, the Zealot and Judas Iscariot, the one who betrayed Him. (Matt 10: 1-7)

Jesus subsequently called Saul (also called Paul) to work for Him uniting him with the mainstream through disciple Ananias. (Acts 9: 1-20; 22: 6-15)

After the crucifixion and accession, and the exit of Judas Iscariot, the Eleven chose Mathias by lot and so he was numbered with the 11 apostles. (Acts 1: 26)

Exhortations, meditation and reflection.

2nd Missionary Journey

The Lord chose another 72 men and sent them out two by two, to go ahead of Him to every town and place where He Himself was about to go…

(Lk 10: 1-12, 17 GNBDK)

Power over demons: oh Lord, revive us again!

The Lord in commissioning the second missionary journey instructed:

"Go on your way; behold, I am sending you like lambs among wolves."

Cure the sick in it AND say to them, 'the kingdom of God is at hand for you.'

Whether you are well received or not, "go into the streets and say, 'the kingdom of God is at hand.'"

It was a successful mission and they rejoiced at their return.

Power to disciples

"Jesus said,

I have observed Satan fall like lighting from the sky. Behold I have given you the power to tread upon serpents and scorpions and upon the full force of the enemy and nothing will harm you."

(Lk 10: 3, 9, 11, 19 NABRE)

Many of us have seen these powers exercised by believers in our lifetime and we need no further evidence that the power has really passed down… We need the power as an integral part of our Christian ministry. Let us crave it, ask for it and the Lord will cause a revival of it, because He knows we need it to function effectively in our various missions.

"As you go, announce this:

'The kingdom of heaven has come near.'" (Matt 10: 7)

The mission

"I have now … filled your mouth with My words.

See, I have appointed you today

over nations and kingdoms

to uproot and teardown,
to destroy and demolish,
to build and plant." (Jer 1: 9, 10)
Who is a Christian?
Exhortations, meditation and reflection.

What is Christianity?

I will answer this question vicariously:

First, every disciple of Jesus Christ is a Christian.

But not every 'Christian' is a disciple. The difference is the extent of conformity with the requirements of discipleship or of followership.

Christianity, therefore, is a fraternity – a way of life. It is more than mere philosophy, an ideologue or that sort of thing.

You can't be a Christian in isolation, just as you cease to be a disciple if you live disparate life, cut away from the master or from other disciples.

The prize of our Christian calling is the kingdom of heaven. See how it works in Matt 20: 1-16: Labourers were hired and worked at different lengths of time, but were paid the same amount for their wages. Yet, the community must eschew envy and rancour.

Apostle Paul puts it this way:

"But now you must also put away all the following: anger, wrath, malice, slander, and filthy language from your mouth. And not lie to one another..."

"Therefore, God's chosen ones, holy and loved, put on heartfelt compassion, kindness, humility, gentleness, and patience, accepting one another and forgiving one another if anyone has a complaint against another. Just as the Lord has forgiven you, so you must also forgive. Above all, put on love – the perfect bond of unity." (Col 3: 8-9, 12-14)

We must learn to give to Caesar what belongs to Caesar and to God total submission and reverence

(Mk 12: 17)

"Turn away from evil and do what is good, and dwell there forever. For the Lord loves justice and will not abandon His faithful ones." (Ps 37: 27-28)

A model or a copycat?

How do you see your Christian life? – Do you often want to be like them? Or you expect them to be like you? Yes, to be like you, because you are like Jesus!

Once you realize that your life is a model for others, a mirror by which others judge themselves a whole lot of responsibility devolves on you. You will make greater effort to be the person you are supposed to be. There will be nothing to bother you because you will expect worse treatment than you get.

Exhortations, meditation and reflection.

"It is enough for a slave to be like the master." So don't look to the world for your values – look to Jesus.

For more on this theme, see "the narrow gate"

"ANYONE who eats My flesh and drinks My blood has eternal life, and I will raise him up on the last day, because My flesh is real food and My blood is real drink." (Jn 6: 54-55 HCSB)

Watchmen, Sentinels

As prophets are the watchmen for the people so are priests, being teachers, are sentinels for them also. And by our baptism in Christ Jesus all disciples share this watchman's responsibility: (Ezk 33: 1-6)

"As for you, son of man, I have made you a watchman for the house of Israel. When you hear a word from My mouth, give them a warning from Me."

(Ezk 33: 7 HCSB)

It has accompanying grace as by this banquet, the diner lives in Christ, and Christ lives in him. (Jn 6: 56)

Christian leaders are commanded to undertake this liturgy "in remembrance of Me" (Lk 22: 19; 1 Cor 11: 24, 25)

It is also a proclamation or gospel of the Lord's death (1 Cor 11: 26), the victory of His salvific ministry (Jesus righteousness) i.e. over the power of sin, Satan and eternal damnation. (The ruler of this world has been judged) (Jn 16: 8-11)

The Living Bread (Jn 6: 51, 54-55)

This is a most important liturgy established by the Lord just a few hours before the commencement of His passion.

In a way, the liturgy is like an emblem or a banner, with which Christ's disciples are associated. It comes in form of a banquet on His body and blood as the main menu 'for the life of the world'

Exhortations, meditation and reflection.

Some disciples found "this teaching too hard" to take in and ceased following Him (Jn 6: 42, 60, 66) for that reason, the liturgy signifies a turning point, a point of separation from those who trusted the Lord completely from those with fickle faith – who deserted:

"they went out from us." (1 Jn 2: 19)

It is sacramental as it connotes that partakers in the banquet are the redeemed whose sins are forgiven and who are pilgrims to everlasting life.

(Jn 6: 40, 47, 54-55, 58)

God's approval for this grace of justification comes in terms of the new covenant sealed with the blood of Jesus. (Jn 6: 27)

Jesus parting words –

To Mary: "woman, behold your son." (Jn 19: 26 NABRE) and

to John (and vicariously to all disciples): "behold your mother" (Jn 19: 27 NABRE)

Oh Mother Mary, you have been bequeathed to us, pray for us, be our helper in times of need. Amen.

At Jesus crucifixion:

At the cross her station keeping[1]

stood the mournful mother weeping

close to Jesus to the last.
"Let me share with you His pain
Who for all our sins was slain
Who for me in torments died."
Through her heart His sorrow sharing
All His bitter anguish bearing
Now at length the sword had passed.
(Jn 19: 26; Lk 2: 35)

1: Stabat Mater. A Roman Catholic dirge at pre-Easter Memorial of Jesus' passion.

Exhortations, meditation and reflection.

God calls you!

If someone told you or you find out by yourself that man sprouts out like grass from the earth and by mutation and adaptation he had become what he is today, won't you be concerned about what he would become tomorrow even after death and what he was before sprouting out?

However, Christian religion has a different explanation for the emergence of man on the earth planet, as the passage quoted from Genesis shows. It explains the origin, purpose and destination of man.

The Creator has designated a role for man in relation to other creatures and also in relation to Himself. If we recognize these and conform, it will be well with us but if we digress or rebel, it is ominous that we would be courting trouble.

"For those He foreknew He also predestined,
to be conformed to the image of His Son...
And those He predestined He also called;
and those He called, He also justified and
those He justified, He also glorified." (Rom 8: 29, 30)

We identify these unique obligation or expectations as divine calls. The average man or woman is expected to fulfil two or more of these roles, namely:

Disciples

My CALL, Your Call.

Nothing is by accident, it is not by chance!

Jer 1:5 Lect "… Before I formed you in the womb I knew you, before you were born I dedicated you a prophet to the nations I appointed you."

i. A call to holiness

"Do you not know that you are the temple of God and that the Spirit of God dwells in you?

If anyone destroys God's temple, God will destroy that person; for the temple of God, which you are, is holy."

(1 Cor 3:16-17 NABRE)

In this context holiness and righteousness are taken to mean the same thing.

Exhortations, meditation and reflection.

"…'Holy, holy, holy is the Lord God almighty,

Who was and who is to come'" (Rev 4: 8 Lect)

- "…be holy in all your conduct for it is written, 'be holy…'" (1 Pt 1: 15)
- Avoid greed and self-indulgence (Matt 23: 25)
- Give, and it shall be given to you

Forgive, and you shall be forgiven; do what is good.

Be merciful as your Father in heaven is merciful (Lk 6: 30, 35, 38)

- Be doers of the word and not hearers only, deluding yourselves (Jas 1: 22 NABRE)
- Yes, these obligations must be met to walk with the Lord. All have sinned and fallen short of the glory of God and not one is free. For the Psalmist says,

"If You kept a record of our sins, who could escape being condemned? But You forgive us, so that we should stand in awe of You." (Ps 130: 3, 4 GNBDK)

- Mercy and forgiveness are proofs of God's holiness (Ezk 36: 2, 4)
- Now the sting of death is sin, (1 Cor 15: 56)

"for the wages of sin is death, but the gift of
God is eternal life in Christ Jesus, our Lord." (Rom 6: 23)
"All unrighteousness is sin,…" (1 Jn 5: 17)
Everyone who commits sin also breaks the law;
Sin is the breaking of law (1 Jn 3: 4)
The core message of Christianity is,
"Repent, for the kingdom of God is at hand" (Mk 1: 15)
"…Look, you were sold for your iniquity and your mother was put away because of your transgressions. (Isa 50: 1)
Exhortations, meditation and reflection.

- Yes, ravaging war, epidemic, pestilence, famine and natural disasters such as flood are some of the rods with which God calls a rebellious people back to order.
- "Repent (seek the Lord) ten times harder (than you have sinned/strayed away from Him) (Bar 4: 28-29)

For He (God, the Father) chose us in Him (Jesus Christ)….. to be holy and blameless in His sight" (Eph 1: 4)

We cannot attain holiness through our individual or intellectual effort alone.

For example, some people who employed their intellect to argue in favour of the state caring for the most vulnerable members of society through welfare schemes were ridiculed by people of another persuasion; they dubbed it as "sharing misery," but when it is a matter of obedience to the Holy God, you will come to realize that the 'foolishness' of God is better than the wisdom of man. (1 Cor 3: 19; 1: 25)

We can attain this personal sanctification by devotion to prayer, reading the scriptures, and meditating on the word of God and doing what we are taught. Living our lives in line with the lives lived by the saints can be a great guide also.

"You must walk and please God…" (1 Thes 4: 1)

In one brief summary, you must live as one "being born again, i.e., believing in Jesus, the light of the world and abandoning wickedness…"

(Jn 3: 3, 5, 18-20; 1 Pt 1: 23; 2 Cor 5: 17)

ii. Called to be in communion (i.e. fellowship) with God

A prophet's call

"If you bring forth the precious without the vile you shall be my mouth piece."

(Jer 15:19, NABRE)

"… if you return, I will restore you; you will stand in My presence. And if you speak noble words, rather than worthless ones, you will be My spokesman."

(Jer 15:19, HCSB)

Exhortations, meditation and reflection.

Mal 2: 10 Have we not all one Father?

Has not one God created us?

Why, then, do we break faith with each other,

Profaning the covenant of our ancestors?

Mal 2: 15 Did He not make them one, with flesh and spirit?

And what does the One require? Godly offspring!

You don't have to go into trance, see visions, perform wonders or speak in tongues to be in communion with God.

You can know that you are in communion with God if you hear, read or share the word of God and the scriptures and meditate on them regularly.

You will have become a citizen of the kingdom of God, no longer tossed around by the waves of ethnic, tribal, class, or racial prejudice but attentive to the needs of others (including strangers) without discrimination, since we all are children of God.

St John gives the formula – love not the world and its distractions and do the will of God (1Jn 2: 15, 17 NABRE)

We can look at this at two levels –

First, at the individual personal level, this is a call to fellowship with God; then at the community or nation level, this is a call to be God's people. We have all been created by God, but like human offspring's, not all of us honour our parents or are dear to them.

Call to fellowship with God "God is faithful; you were called by Him into fellowship with His

Son Jesus Christ our Lord" (2 Cor 1:18 HCSB)

All who fear the Lord and obey His commandments and precepts, are, indeed, children of God! They can call God, *Abba, Father*!

Adam, our pristine father, was in fellowship with God but hid himself from God:

"I was afraid because I was naked, so I hid" (Gen 3: 10)

Exhortations, meditation and reflection.

There is no hiding place for sin and it separates us from the holy God who created us for communion with Himself. Why would anyone forsake (to enjoy) that sacred communion with God?

"so we are all present before God,…" (Acts 10: 33)

The sinner too, is called to communion with God! But he must first walk away from past wickedness and evil. Jesus explains that He has not come to call the righteous but sinners to repentance. (Lk 5:32)

Two such sinners responded – as models for us all:

First, a woman heard about Jesus. The woman, "who was a sinner found out that Jesus was reclining at table" in the house of Simon, a Pharisee. There she demonstrated her repentance. (Lk 7: 36-50) In the second episode Zaccheus, rich but infamous, heard also that Jesus was passing by, but Jesus saw repentance in his heart.

Jesus was unequivocal in stipulating the terms for His followers:

"Whoever wishes to come after Me must deny himself,
Take up his cross and follow Me." (Mk 8: 34)

iii. Call to discipleship

It was Joshua, Moses assistant and successor, who made the declaration:

"for me and my household, we will serve the Lord." (Jos 24: 2, 3) You may have heard about the call of Elisha by Elija (actually Elija acted on God's command) (1 Kgs 19: 16): Lot… by Abraham, Aaron… by Moses; Andrew and Simon, James and his brother John, by Jesus. These are truly ecstatic and dramatic. But look at Nathaniel's call ("come and see!"), it was more subtle, yet solemn.

Discipleship – for succor

Jesus beckons, and promises:

"Come to Me, all of you who are weary and burdened, and I will give you rest … take up My yoke and learn from Me, … and you will find rest for yourselves. For My yoke is easy and My burden is light." (Matt 11:28-30, HCSB)

Exhortations, meditation and reflection.

Faithful and Prudent Servant:

"Stay awake!" (Matt 24:42)

"Be Prepared …" (Matt 24:44)

"…You have the word of eternal life" (Jn 6: 68)

Of course your dedication is not in vain: 'a hundred times' reward (Matt 19: 29)

You must be steadfast in your fellowship - "neither hot nor cold is not acceptable" –

(Rev 3:16) for example, some complained, "This teaching is hard: who can accept it?" (Jn 6: 60)

Some who don't believe …

And the Lord's response: "But there are some among you who don't believe (Jn 6: 64)

Could that be you?

He who perseveres to the end receives the crown (Rev 3:21)

Your call and its purpose is beyond doubt because He has said it:

- "Go, make disciples of all the nations…" (Matt 28: 18, 20) so once you are steady in the saddle as a disciple, you must go forth and make disciples of others not your personal disciple but disciples of the Lord Jesus Christ. "for we are God's co-workers…

I have laid a foundation as a skilled master builder, and another builds on it. For no one can lay any other foundation than what has been laid down.

That foundation is Jesus Christ." (1 Cor 3: 9, 10-11)

Your Gifts – or the graces of God in your life should not lead you into pride:

"Now, there are different gifts, but the same spirit. There are different ministries but the same Lord. And there are different activities, but the same God activates each gift in each person." (1 Cor 12: 4-6)

"Now you are the body of Christ, and individually members of it." (1 Cor 12: 27)

Exhortations, meditation and reflection.

Inadequate to the task? Leave that to the Master. He will convert your availability to capability. Moses complained of his stammering, Samuel dreaded Saul Jeremiah and Gideon complained about their youthfulness; yet they succeeded.

"If you are ridiculed for the name of Christ, you are blessed,…" (1 Pt 4: 14)

"A slave is not greater than the master; the messenger than the one who sent him" (Jn 13:16)

And even "the dead who die in the Lord from now on are blessed" (Rev 14: 13)

No looking back

"But Jesus said to him, 'no one who puts his hand to the plough and looks back is fit for the kingdom of God'" (Lk 9: 62)

There are three levels of witnessing – with your words, with your deeds and sometimes, inevitably with your blood.

iv. Called to bear fruit

"I chose you from the world to go and bear fruit." (Jn 15: 16)

"You did not choose Me, but I chose you. I appointed you that you should go and produce fruit and that your fruit should remain, so that whatever you ask the Father in My name, He will give you." (Jn 15: 16)

- The word of God has been planted in you; it is the seed and you are the soil on which it is planted. The Lord expects a harvest of a hundred fold, sixty fold from the good soil (Matt 13:23).
- Jesus makes it clear that – "not everyone who says to Me, 'Lord, Lord!' will enter the kingdom of heaven" (Matt 7: 21)
- "'The dead who die in the Lord from now on are blessed' 'yes! Says the spirit', 'let them rest from their labours for their works follow them.'" (Rev 14: 13)

Exhortations, meditation and reflection.

- JESUS is "the way, the truth and the life." Whoever wants to be a disciple of His must first desire a fellowship with God. The Lord may then appoint such as a shepherd of some of His flock:

And again:

- "I chose you before I formed you in the womb;
I set you apart before you were born.

I appointed you a prophet to the nations." (Jer 1: 5)
And yet again:

- "…I watch over My word to accomplish it." (Jer 1: 12)
- Jesus is the vine, His Father the vine keeper, you are the branches. The Father prunes the branch that it may bear fruit but the axe is on all branches that do not bear fruit (Jn 15:5). Because cut away from Jesus, you can do nothing!

Each person to mind his own business and hold the fort. Every vocation is important, if well performed.

Jesus says, "what is that to you?" if I want him to be (this) and you to be (that) (Jn 21: 22)

He reminds us of their common denominator – SERVICE to the people of God.

"You know that the leaders of this world lord it on their people; but for you,

it shall not be so. Whoever wants to be great shall be the servant of all;

whoever wants to be first shall be slave." Is that clearly understood and accepted by you?

To really bear much fruit calls for sacrifices –

"If a grain of wheat does not fall and die it cannot bear much fruit"

Suffering teaches oneself endurance, endurance leads to perfection David would not give a gift to God that costs him nothing.

Exhortations, meditation and reflection.

Let your righteousness (your faith as a Christian, Muslim, whatever) beam brilliant rays of its goodness beyond the precincts of your assembly, sanctuary, mosque, church, etc. Go all out and bear fruit!

"The Lord measures our perfection neither by the multitude nor the magnitude of our deeds, but by the manner in which we perform them." St John of the cross.

That explains why of all the patriarchs, prophets and kings up to the time of John the Baptist, not one was greater than he, yet the least in the kingdom of heaven is greater than he. (Matt 11:11; Lk 7:28)

v. Called to feed the flock – As pastors, bishops, general overseers, rulers, etc.

"Simon… feed My lambs,… shepherd My sheep…, feed My sheep" (Jn 21: 15-17).

That is your mandate, a sacred duty – feed with the physical food and spiritually with words of truth and encouragement as the Master Himself did. Remember always the One who gave you the mandate on whose behalf you are serving – who is the chief shepherd – the shepherd of all (Ps 23: 1-5) and be like Him to the flock you pasture.

The leadership of the Christian faith had descended from Simon Peter and the Apostles to you today at this hour, so too, you, the political leader of the people of God – you are now in the seat of Moses! And you have the charismof David to sway your generation. So do it well – for you are serving the Lord!

"Whatever you did not do to the least of My brothers that you did not do to Me" (Matt 25:45)

As the Father sent Me so am I sending you… (Jn 20: 21)

Elisha in his service said, "…Give to the people to eat, they ate and were filled."

(2 Kgs 4: 42) and he blessed the resource that thus ransomed the prophets widow's son from slavery

(2 Kgs 4: 1-)

David ensured that bread was available for his officers and men; Christ, the good shepherd started his ministry by providing wine at Cana, later he fed 5,000 and 4,000; after His resurrection He fed Peter and his colleagues who were about backsliding with grilled fish.

Exhortations, meditation and reflection.

Feeding, of course, is not restricted to physical food but is all embracing, encouragement, and material welfare.

Apostle Peter says "I exhort (you) the elders among you to shepherd God's flock among you, not overseeing out of compulsion but freely according to God's will; not for the money but eagerly." (1 Pt 5: 1, 4)

And Apostle Paul writes

"An overseer... must be above reproach... self-controlled, sensible, respectable, hospitable, an able teacher, not addicted to wine, not a bully but gentle, not quarrelsome, not greedy,..." (1 Tim 3: 2-3) And as a "man of God... fight the good fight for the faith" (1 Tim 6: 11-12).

Then go out there and bear fruit – fruit of repentance, contrition; the fruit of self-less love, compassion and generosity.

What about the fruits of your growth in the spirit – faith, hope, love, endurance, charity, patience, wisdom, understanding, knowledge and fear of God, self-control?

Let the world see your good work so it may give praise to our Father in heaven.

Lead people to Jesus and raise them for the kingdom.

Finally, be guided by what the prophet says,

Do not feed yourselves – rather, feed the flock! Do not feed off the sheep's milk, wear their wool, slaughter their fatlings, but seek and bring back the strayed and the lost; tend and heal the sick. Don't rule with violence and cruelty. The Lord will demand accountability from you! (Ezk 34: 1-10)

And again,

"Woe to the shepherds who destroy and scatter the flocks of My pasture – oracle of the Lord." (Jer 23: 1 NABRE)

Hearken to the command of the Lord, ('Comfort, comfort My people'), says your God" (Isa 40:1 HCSB)

vi. Called to Secular life

As business men and women, military men and women, professionals – academicians, public servants, teachers, engineers, doctors, scientists, technocrats, artisans, leaders of government and legislature, etc.,

Exhortations, meditation and reflection.

"Based on the gift each one has received, use it to serve others as good managers of the varied grace of God." (1 Pt 4: 10)

The Church has been established because of you! You are called to enter the kingdom of God; that the Way you live your life may be a trustworthy witness to the gospel ethos.

You are called to be the conscience of society, hold dear your Christian values – be the lamp to your community – a light that dispels the darkness of error, falsehood and wickedness.

"Your light must shine in the sight of men… so that seeing your good works, they give the praise to your Father in heaven." (Matt 5: 16)

You are the salt of the world (or at least to your generation) but if the salt loses its taste, it is good for nothing.

You serve the yeast of the kingdom – that adds value – righteousness, truth and praise of God to the communal endeavours.

vii. Call to be God's people

"Our soul waits for the Lord, who is our help and our shield, for in Him our hearts rejoice; in His holy name we trust" (Ps 33:30)

"Blessed is the nation whose God is the Lord, the people He has chosen for His own inheritance." (Ps 33: 12)

"This is My beloved Son; listen to Him" (Matt 17: 5; Mk 9: 7)

On three memorable occasions the gospel recorded the release of the voice of God commending Jesus to mankind as our mentor, teacher, and model of perfection (light of the world) (Jn 8: 12)

Political leaders of God's own people have enormous responsibility in this regard. They have to lead the people in "a pilgrim fellowship"[3] in walking this path of Righteousness.

3: Pope Francis: "overcoming indifference and win peace" re. celebration of the 49th World Day of Peace, Jan 1, 2016.

Exhortations, meditation and reflection.

For forty years, Israel sojourned in the desert learning how to walk with the Lord and raising a new generation in righteousness. It was certainly not an easy road to walk but at the end bliss awaited those who persevered.

That was Zion, but today, it is not so reassuring that the people still wished to be or remain 'the people of God'.

The Lord insistently calls us to, "be attentive to Me, My people; for teaching shall go forth from Me, and My judgement, as light to the peoples."

(Isa 51: 4) NABRE

The holy scriptures tell us that:

"Righteousness exalts a nation but sin is a disgrace to any people"

(Prov 14: 34)

Unbridled nationalism (like in Hitler's Reich) and the blindness and the prejudice of tribalism, ethnicism and racism will ultimately lead to unrighteousness (like hatred of foreigners) since such bigots fail to recognize the universal (i.e., divine) brotherhood of man.

Lazy gods

I wish these unrighteous 'gods' were at least as powerful as the sons of men! Then, they would not need ghostly humans to help them fight their human foes! Dogs don't eat dogs; then, man would not have to fight and ruin a fellow-human who could be an innocent neighbour!

We are all created by God, thus all who answer the divine call are God's people. Each nation or people have to make the choice explicitly or deliberately. Such people or nation must put on the whole amour of God; love one another as God (in Christ) loved us. They should not relent to be their brother's keeper – i.e., lend and share with members who are in dire or higher need than themselves. They should not be untouched by what their neighbours are going through, alleviating their pains and ameliorating their condition:

"When I was hungry you fed me… naked, you clothed me… in prison,…sick, you visited and comforted Me."(Matt 25:4:35-36)

Exhortations, meditation and reflection.

The founding fathers of the USA inserted in their banner, "In God, we trust." Then, Uncle Sam, was known as 'God's own country', an epithet to be coveted.

"But you are a chosen race, a royal priesthood, a holy nation, a people for His possession, so that you may proclaim the praises of the One who called you out of darkness into His marvellous light."

"Once you were not a people, but now you are God's people; you had not received mercy, but now you have received mercy." (1 Pt 2: 9, 10)

Stop! Jesus, the light of the world, beckons on peoples and nations at this hour to, "come to Me…" (Matt 11: 28)

CHAPTER 17

Salvation:Orthodoxy, Heresy, and Apostasy

Chair of Moses:

"The Scribes and the Pharisees are seated in the chair of Moses. Therefore, do whatever they tell you, and observe it. But don't do what they do, because they don't practise what they teach." (Matt 23: 2-3)

Chair of Peter:

"And I also say to you that you are Peter,

and on this rock I will build My church,

and the forces of hades will not overpower it.

I will give you the keys of the kingdom of heaven, ..."

(Matt 16: 18-19 HCSB)

Peter appointed shepherd

"Simon, son of John... feed My lambs..." (Jn 21: 15-17 NABRE)

The Antichrist

"They went out from us, but they did not belong to us; for if they had belonged to us, they would have remained with us. However, they went out so that it might be made clear that none of them belongs to us."

"Who is the liar, if not the one who denies that Jesus is the Messiah?...

I have written these things to you about those who are trying to deceive you."

(1 Jn 2: 19, 22, 26)

"Many deceivers...; they do not confess the coming of Jesus Christ in the flesh. This is the deceiver and the antichrist."

"Anyone who does not remain in Christ's teaching but goes beyond it, does not have God... do not receive him into your home..."

(2 Jn 1: 7, 9-10 HCSB)

Strange teachings lead people astray.

"Don't be led astray by various kinds of strange teachings; for it is good for the heart to be established by grace and not by foods,..." (Heb 13: 9 HCSB)

Presumptive Prophecy:

"WHEN a prophet speaks in the Lord's name and the message does not come true or is not fulfilled, that is a message the Lord has not spoken. The prophet has spoken presumptuously.

Do not be afraid of him." (Deut 18: 22 HCSB)

Paul: On False Apostles

"...those who seek a pretext for being regarded as we are in the mission..." "...such people are false apostles, deceitful workers, who masquerade as apostles of Christ." "... Satan masquerades as an angel of light. So it is not strange that his ministers also masquerade as ministers of righteousness..."

(2 Cor 11: 12-14 NABRE)

Read also Col 2: 2-4 NRSV-CI

Jesus is divine (Col 2: 8-9 HCSB):

"Be careful that no one takes you captive through philosophy and empty deceit... and not based on Christ. For the entire fullness of God's nature dwells bodily in Christ."

"Let no one disqualify you, insisting on ascetic practices and the worship of angels, claiming access to a visionary realm and inflated without cause by his unspiritual mind." (Col 2: 18 HCSB)

FALSE PROPHECIES AND FAKE PROPHETS.

"In the beginning of the reign of Zedekiah, king of Judah, in the 5th month of the 4th year, Hananiah the prophet, son of Azzur,... (Proclaimed):

'Thus says the Lord of hosts,… I have broken the yoke of the king of Babylon. Within two years I will restore… all the vessels… Nebuchadnezzar… carried away to Babylon… Jaconiah son of Jehoiakim… and all the exiles… I will bring back…' Thereupon, Hananiah… took the yoke bar from the neck of Jeremiah… and broke it.

After… the word of the Lord came to Jeremiah:

'by breaking a wooden yoke bar, you make an iron yoke!…

… they shall serve him; even the wild animals I have given him… …Hananiah! The Lord has not sent you… I am sending you from the face of the earth this very year you shall die…'

Hananiah the prophet died in the 7th month in that year" (i.e. two months after his false prophecy) (Jer 28: 1-17)

A similar prophetic disunity occurred in Bethel when a man of God from Judah came to Bethel when Jeroboam was incensing the alter and prophesied the birth of Josiah who will unleash the wrath of God on the fake priests. This old prophet deceived and misled the man of God by a fake prophesy, and this caused the life of the man of God. (1 Kgs 13: 1-30)

Straying from the truth (Js 5: 19-20)

"… Know that whoever turns a sinner from the error of his way will save his life from death and cover a multitude of sins." (Js 5: 20

One Foundation: Jesus

"… But each one must be
careful how he builds on it. For no one can lay
any other foundation than what has been laid down.
That foundation is Jesus Christ." (1 Cor 3:11 IICSB)
Power to bind and to loosen
"Blessed are you, Simon son of Jonah. For flesh and blood has not revealed this to you,…

And I say to you, you are Peter, and upon this rock I will build My church, and the gates of the nether world shall not prevail against it.

I will give you the keys to the kingdom of heaven. Whatever you bind on earth shall be bound in heaven, and whatever you lose on earth shall be loosed in heaven."

(Matt 16: 17-19 NABRE)

Be One!

The Lord asked the Father: "... **Sanctify them by the truth...**"

"Holy Father, protect them by Your name... so that they may be one as We are one. Sanctify them by the truth; Your word is truth."

"I pray not only for these, but also for those who believe in Me through their message: may they all be one." (Jn 17: 11, 17, 20-21 HCSB)

Another gospel? A curse be on the preacher!

"I am surprised at you! In no time at all you are deserting the one who called you by the grace of Christ, and are accepting another gospel. Actually, there is no "other gospel", but I say this because there are some people who are upsetting you and trying to change the gospel of Christ.

But even if we or an angel from heaven should preach to you a gospel that is different from the one we preached to you, **may he be condemned to hell!**" (Gal 1: 6-8 GNBDK)

"...the gospel that I preach is not of human origin." "...it was Jesus Christ Himself who revealed it to me." (Gal 1: 11, 12 GNBDK)

The gospel – a trammel, not to be cast away:

"Woe to those who call evil good and good evil,
who substitute darkness for light and light for darkness,
who substitute bitter for sweet
and sweet for bitter.
...who are wise in their own opinion

and clever in their own sight
…heroes at drinking wine,
who are fearless at mixing beer,
who acquit the guilty for a bribe
and deprive the innocent of justice." (Isa 5: 20-23 HCSB)

Things that cause sin

"Woe to the world because of things that cause sin! Such things must come, but woe to the one through whom they come!" (Matt 18: 7 NABRE)

The true God and eternal life

"…that the Son of God, has come and has given us understanding so that we may know the True One. We are in the True One – that is, in His Son Jesus Christ. He is the true God and eternal life." (1 Jn 5: 20 HCSB)

THEY WENT OUT FROM US

"They went out from us… not really of our number; if they had been, they would have remained with us. Their desertion shows that **none of them was of our number.**" (1 Jn 2: 19 NABRE)

Pursue Peace!

"Pursue peace with everyone, and holiness without it no one will see the Lord.

Make sure… that no root of bitterness springs up, causing trouble, and by it, defiling many." (Heb 12: 14, 15 HCSB)

"But avoid irreverent, empty speech, for this will produce… even greater godlessness." (2 Tim 2: 16 HCSB)

Some men from Judea (an instance of presumptive teaching)

"Some men came down from Judea and began to teach the brothers, 'unless you are circumcised according to the custom prescribed by Moses, you cannot be saved!" (Acts 15: 1 HCSB)

Apostasy

"During that time there was a major disturbance about the way". Read Acts 19: 23-41 for how Demetrius was able to mobilize some people for a major uproar against the faith.

Paul, to the Ephesians: **Be on the alert!**

"I testified to both Jews and Greeks about repentance toward God and faith in our Lord Jesus..."

"Be on your guard for yourselves and for all the flock that the Holy Spirit has appointed you to as overseers, to shepherd the church of God, which He purchased with His own blood. I know ... that savage wolves will come in among you, not sparing the flock. And men will rise up from your own number with deviant doctrines to lure the disciples into following them. Therefore, be on the alert..." (Acts 20: 21, 28-31)

The apostasy of the Jews from Asia

Read about this also in Acts 21: 21-23: 11; 23: 12-24: 27.

Miracles wrought through Paul

"God was performing extraordinary miracles by Paul's hands, so that even facecloths or work aprons that had touched his skin were brought to the sick, and the disease left them and the evil spirits came out of them."

(Acts 19: 11-12 HCSB)

But who are you?

"I know Jesus, and I recognise Paul – but who are you?" (Acts 19: 15 HCSB)

The Earliest Evangelism Message.

The earliest teaching of the Apostles, from the day of Pentecost upwards centred on –

1. The God of Abraham, Isaac and Jacob "glorified His servant Jesus…, the Author of Life" whom "you put to death, but God raised Him from the dead; of this we are witnesses." (Acts 2: 32; 3: 13, 15 NABRE)
2. "Repent, be baptized… receive the gift of the Holy Spirit." (Acts 2: 38 HCSB)
3. Know with certainty that God has made this Jesus … both Lord and Messiah! (Acts 2: 36)
4. "… He (Jesus) is the One appointed by God to be the judge of the living and the dead… through His name everyone who believes in Him will receive forgiveness of sins." (Acts 10: 42-43 HCSB)

Further accounts of the teachings of the Apostles can be found in the books of the New Testament other than the Gospels.

Prophets and pastors doing their own thing.

"The Lord says,
- 'The prophets and the priests are godless; I have caught them doing evil in the temple itself.

The paths they follow will be slippery and dark; I will make them stumble and fall. I am going to bring disaster on them;…'"

"…they help people to do wrong, so that no one stops doing what is evil…" (Jer 23: 11-12, 14 GNBDK)

- "The Lord said, 'I did not send these prophets, but even so they went. I did not give them any message, but still they spoke in My name.'" (Jer 23: 21 GNBDK)
- "I am against those prophets who take each other's words and proclaim them as My message. I am also against those prophets who speak their own words and claim they came from Me." (Jer 23: 30-31 GNBDK)

- **IF** – "But if a prophet presumes to speak a word in My name that I have not commanded, or speaks in the name of other gods, that prophet shall die."

(Deut 18: 20 NABRE)

ADDITIONAL RESOURCES

17. Orthodoxy

Jesus the Master Plan of our faith

1 Cor 3: 10 "...I (Paul) have laid a foundation as a skilled master builder, and another builds on it.

But each one must be careful how he builds on it."

1 Cor 3: 11 "For no one can lay any other foundation than what has been laid down, that foundation is Jesus Christ."

1 Jn 4: 3 **the antichrist**... their teaching belongs to the world; and the world listens to them.

4: 6 we belong to God and anyone who knows God listens to us,

while anyone who does not belong to God refuse to hear us. This is how we know the Spirit of truth and the spirit of deceit.

One Causing Another to Lose Faith: (see also Matt 18: 6-9, Lk 17: 1-2)

Mk 9: 42 "if anyone should cause one of these little ones to lose his GNBDK faith in Me, it would be better for that person to have a large millstone tied round his neck and be thrown into the sea."

: 43 "so if your hand makes you to lose... (the kingdom) cut it off!..."

On true and false doctrine:

Matt 6: 22, 23 "The lamp of the body is the eye. If your eye is sound,

NABRE your whole body will be filled with light; but if your eye is bad, your whole body will be in darkness. And if the light in you is darkness, how great will the darkness be."

THE WORD OF GOD

Isa 55: 10 "For just as rain and snow fall from heaven and do not return there without saturating the earth and making it germinate and sprout, and providing seed to sow and food to eat,

: 11 so My word that comes from My mouth

will not return to Me empty,

but it will accomplish what I please

and will prosper in what I send it to do."
Preserve justice, do what is right!
Isa 56: 1 "Preserve justice and do what is right,
for My salvation is coming soon,
and My righteousness will be revealed."

False Prophecies

Jer 14: 14 HCSB
"But the Lord said to me,
'these prophets are prophesying a lie in My name.
I did not send them, nor did I command them or speak to them.
They are prophesying to you a false vision, worthless divination,
the deceit of their own minds.'"
FALSE PROPHETS
Jer 23: 11 "because both prophet and priest are ungodly,…
HCSB : 12 Therefore… I will bring disaster on them,…"
23: 21 "I did not send these prophets,
yet they ran with a message!
I did not speak to them,
yet they prophesied."
: 25 "I have heard what the prophets who prophesy a lie in My
name have said, 'I had a dream! I had a dream!'
: 28 The prophet who has only a dream should recount the
dream, but the one who has My word should speak My word
truthfully, for what is a straw compared to grain? – this is the Lord's
declaration."
Sound doctrine or myths and fables: On which side are you?
2 Tm 4: 3-4, 5 NKJV
: 3 "For the time will come when they will not endure sound
doctrine, but according to their own desires,… they will heap up for
themselves teachers;…
: 4 turn their ears away from the truth, and be turned aside to
fables."

: 5 "But you be watchful… endure afflictions…"

The essence of sound doctrine

"Beloved you must say what is consistent with sound doctrine…" (Tit 2: 1 Lect)
"… teaching what is good,…
… so that the word of God may not be discredited.
… showing yourself as a model of good deeds in every respect
… so that the opponent will be put to shame
without anything bad to say about us." (Tit 2: 1-8 Lect)
"Trust the Lord with all your hearts,
and do not rely on your own understanding."
(Pro 3: 5 HCSB)

True faith, tradition and dogma – a slippery path.

"They also presented false witnesses who said, '…for we heard him say that Jesus, the Nazarene, will destroy this place and change the customs that Moses handed down to us'"
(Acts 6: 13, 14 HCSB)
"Trust in the Lord with all your heart,
on your own intelligence do not rely." (Pro 3: 5 NABRE)

No perfect Knowledge yet.

"For we know partially and we prophesy partially…
At present we see indistinctly, as in a mirror.
But then face to face.
At present I know partially;
then I shall know fully…" (1 Cor 13: 9, 12 Lect)
TRADITION AND SIN
So, the Pharisees and Scribes questioned Him, 'Why do your disciples not follow the tradition of the elders but instead eat a meal with unclean hands?'
(Mk 7: 1-13)

Response:

This people honour Me with their lips,
but their hearts are far from Me;
in vain do they worship Me,
teaching as doctrines human precepts. (Isa 29: 13)

"How well you have set aside the commandment of God in order to uphold human tradition!"

JESUS: On False Teaching

"… Pharisees and Scribes… said … 'your disciples break the tradition of the elders… not wash hands when they eat…'"

Jesus "said to them… you break the commandment of God… Hypocrites, well did Isaiah prophesy about you… '…in vain do they worship me, teaching as doctrine human precepts.'"

Then His disciples… said to Him, 'Do you know the Pharisees took offence (at)… what you said?'

"He said in reply, 'Every plant that My heavenly Father has not planted will be uprooted.'"

"'… they are blind guides…'" (Matt 15: 1-2, 3-9, 12-14 NABRE)

"He also told them a parable: 'can the blind guide the blind? Won't they fall into a pit?'"(Lk 6: 39 HCSB)

FALSE PROPHETS (See also: False Teachings)

Matt 7: 15 Jesus says "Beware of false prophets who came to you in sheep's clothing but inwardly are ravaging wolves."

Matt 7: 16 "You'll recognise them by their fruit…" (ditto for 7: 20)

(Matt 15: 12-14 HCSB)

"'Every plant that My heavenly Father didn't plant will be uprooted.

Leave them alone! They are blind guides. And if the blind guide the blind both will fall into a pit.'"

The Antichrist

Lord, bring light into our darkness.

2 Jn 1: 7 Antichrist against the anointed One;

willmake a pretence of religion…

theantichrist will want to spiritualize Jesus and deny His incarnationagainst the church.

Matt 24: 5 Many will come attempting to impersonate Jesus Christ!

Mk 13: 21 'Look, the Messiah is here …' – do not believe; it will even try the faithof the chosen

Mk 13: 20 The Lord will shorten his days to save mankind

1 Jn 2: 18 Many antichrists have appeared – heretics

1 Jn 2: 20 He is a'Liar', the one denying Christ is the antichrist.

1 Jn 4: 2, 3 _ _ _ _ _ _ _ _ _ _ _ _

2 Thes 2: 3 The lawless one (son of destruction),Law-denying, not…

Remain in Christ's Teaching

"Anyone who does not remain in Christ's teaching but goes beyond it, does not have God. The one who remains in that teaching, …has both the Father and the Son." (2 Jn 1: 9 HCSB)

Don't revel in being a Diotrephes! (3 Jn 1: 9)

Impurity and error

"For our exhortation didn't come from error or impurity or an intent to deceive instead, …we speak not to please men, but rather God, who examines our hearts." (1 Thes 2: 3-4)

Judgement, Mercy and Fidelity

"… you pay tithes of mint, dill and cumin, and have neglected the weightier things of the law: judgement and mercy and fidelity.

But these you should have done without neglecting the others." (Matt 23: 23-24 Lect)

Lk 11: 42/ Matt 23: 23 NABRE

Mightier things.

"You neglected the mightier things of the law: judgement and mercy and fidelity…"

False Teaching

"Now the Spirit explicitly says that in later times some will depart from the faith, paying attention to deceitful spirits and the teachings of demons."

(1 Tim 4: 1 HCSB)

One Lord, one faith, one hope

"Therefore, I… urge you to walk worthy of the calling you have received, with all humility and gentleness, with patience, accepting one another in love, diligently keeping the unity of the Spirit with the peace that binds us."

"There is one body and one Spirit – just as you were called to one hope at your calling – one Lord, one faith, one baptism, one God and Father of all – who is above all and through all and in all." (Eph 4: 1-6 HCSB)

Jesus "in the flesh" – the antichrist.

"Many deceivers have gone out into the world; they do not confess the coming of Jesus Christ in the flesh. This is the deceiver and the antichrist." (2 Jn 1:7 HCSB)

Fanciful Visions!

"Both prophet and priest are godless!

In My very house I find their wickedness –

oracle of the Lord."

"… they speak visions from their own fancy,

not from the mouth of the Lord."

"they say, …to everyone who walks in

hardness of heart, 'no evil shall overtake you.'"

(Jer 23: 11, 16-17 NABRE)

My people perish for lack of knowledge.(Hos 6: 2)

Add not, nor subtract

(Deut 4: 2) In your observance of the commandments… you shall not add to or subtract from it. Observe them CAREFULLY…

Individual interpretations

(Isa 29: 31) They paid lip service to the observance of God's commandments substituting their own ingenious interpretations and clever arguments to void the will of God

The Magisterium: "…do whatever they tell you, and observe it, but…" (Matt 23: 3 HCSB)

(Rev 2: 2) "You have tested those calling themselves apostles and are not,…"

(Mk 12: 28-34) The most important commandment of the law: Love God, love your neighbour as yourself.

Right leadership

Those who are wise will shine… and those who lead many to righteousness, like the stars forever and ever.(Dan 12: 3 HCSB)

Accord; be united!

(1 Cor 1: 10) Now, I urge you… that all of you AGREE in what you say… no divisions… be united with the same understanding and the same conviction.

In the name of Jesus Christ…

"Teacher, we saw someone driving out demons in your name and we tried to prevent him because he does not follow us."

"Don't stop him," said Jesus… (Mk 9: 39 Lect)

Food does not defile.

"… Listen to Me, all of you, and understand:

Nothing that goes into a person from outside can defile him,

but the things that come out of a person are what defile him."

(Mk 7: 14-15)

The Fruit: life, or the destruction of lives?

"The fruit of righteousness is a tree of life,

but violence takes lives away." (Prov 11: 30 NRSV-CI)

Guard the truth.

"Be on your guard for yourselves and for all the flock... to shepherd the church of God... I know that... savage wolves will come in among you, not sparing the flock. And men will rise up from your own number with deviant doctrines to lure disciples into following them."
(Acts 20: 28-30 HCSB)

Consulting Mediums and Spiritists

"Do not turn to mediums or consult spiritists, or you will be defiled by them. I am Yahweh your God." (Lev 19: 31)
Spirit of promiscuity
"My people consult their wooden and their divining rods inform them. For a spirit of promiscuity leads them astray; they act promiscuously in disobedience to their God.

My friends, do not believe every spirit, but test the spirits to determine if they are from God, because many false prophets have gone out into the world."
(Tit 2: 13, ...)
Exhortation, Meditation and Reflection

On development (of doctrine):

St Vincent of Lepins: "Is there to be development of religion in the church of Christ? Certainly, there is to be development."
"... but it must be development of the faith, not alteration of the faith. Development means that each thing exists to be itself whilst alteration means that a thing is changed from one thing into another..."
The Word: Let it quench your thirst, and not your thirst the word.
Excerpts from A Commentary by St. Ephrem, Deacon:

"Lord, who can comprehend even one of your words? We lose more of it than we grasp,... For God's word offers different facets according to the capacity of the listener, and the Lord has portrayed His message in many colours, so that whoever gazes upon it can see in it what suits him within it. He has buried manifold treasures, so that each of us might grow rich in seeking them out."

"And so whenever anyone discovers some part of the treasure, he should not think that he has exhausted God's word. Instead, he should feel that this is all that he was able to find of the wealth contained in it..."

"Be glad then that you are overwhelmed, and do not be saddened because He has overcome you. A thirsty man is happy when he is drinking, and he is not depressed because he cannot exhaust the spring. So let this spring quench your thirst, and not your thirst the spring..."

"Be thankful then for what you have received, and do not be saddened at all that such an abundance still remains. What you have received and attained is your present share, while what is left will be your heritage. For what you could not take at one time because of your weakness, you will be able to grasp at another if you only persevere. So do not foolishly try to drain in one draught what cannot be consumed all at once, and do not cease out of faint heartedness from what you will be able to absorb as time goes on."

Abstain from heresy

St Ignatius of Antioch[1]: "I strongly urge you,... to be nourished exclusively on Christ's fare, abstaining from the alien food that is heresy."

Heresy according to Fr Al Luer is a spiritual JunkFood causing spiritual Anorexia.

1: St Ignatius of Antioch, Letter to the Trallians
"ANYONE who does not remain
in Christ's teaching but goes beyond it,
does not have God. The one who remains
in that teaching, this one has both the Father and the Son."

(2 Jn 1: 9 HCSB)

Blind guides: Brood of vipers. (Matt 23: 15-17 HCSB)

"… You travel over land and sea to make one proselyte, and when he becomes one, you make him twice as fit for hell as you are!"

"Woe to you blind guides who say 'whoever takes an oath by the sanctuary, it means nothing. But whoever takes an oath by the gold of the sanctuary is bound by his oath.' Blind fools! Which is greater, the gold or the sanctuary that sanctified the gold?"

A block cannot resist the storm flood standing alone – a tree does not make a forest – if you are a disciple your strength will be in belonging to the authentic body of disciples. "They went out from us, but they did not belong to us..." And if you are not with us, then you are against us. ( ) certainly, if your fellowship is not with the Apostles and your teaching is not rooted in Christ, It must be in the Devil, meaning that you are an antichrist;

"Snakes! Brood of vipers! How can you escape being condemned to hell?" (Matt 23: 33)

A warning against presumption.

"None is greater than Me!" "My congregation is the biggest." "I know it all!" Remember the gate is wide and the road broad that leads to destruction; many go through it.

Those are symptomatic of the underlying malaise that had continued to drive a wedge between the efforts at arriving at a kerygmatic creed for our faith.

It was not Martin Luther who first started it, only the wound has refused to heal, indeed, it has festered. The Roman Catholic Church was similarly accused by the Eastern (Orthodox) church for the latter's refusal to continue with a united front. But even before these, Moses had been rebuffed, "you have gone too far! Everyone in the entire community is holy…" (Num 16: 3)

Then, God showed the difference; He can do it again!

Thus, as it was, so it may ever be! But that does not provide us an alibi for saying different opposing things about the faith we profess: about the teaching and preaching of Jesus and His Apostles. Who gains by this scenario other than the evil one?

Exhortation, Meditation and Reflection

We should put our differences aside and agree on the authenticity of our faith and who the teacher of last resort is among us; for continual guidance and clarification (orthodoxy) who is that person or institution?

"Therefore, whoever thinks he is standing secure should take care not to fall."

(1 Cor 10: 12)

Apostles and disciples-in-communion.

Presumptive Teaching
Speculative Teaching
Tendentious Teaching
Demonic Teaching

Certainly all these cannot be right! Or what would one then make of the authentic teaching of the Lord Himself and of His duly commissioned, well groomed and anointed Apostles and disciples-in-communion? I mean disciples who shared in the faith and teaching of St Peter, and the other Apostles and disciples of Jesus who are a communion with him, who have not broken faith or trust on the kernels of the faith?

"The Church":

"I assure you: Whatever you bind on earth is already bound in heaven." (Matt 18: 17, 18 HCSB)

Certainly, Jesus did not imply the church of Satan (Rev.) or churches based on tendentious, speculative or presumptive teachings discussed above. He was referring to the church He established Himself (as per Matt 16: 17-19) "built on the foundation of the apostles and prophets, with Christ Jesus Himself as the cornerstone." (Eph 2: 20 HCSB)

The Darkness of Heresy vis-à-vis the light of truth

In Genesis, darkness and bleakness co-existed before light and life. God has delighted in giving mankind day and night, male and female. So long as there is the truth, there must be falsehood for the difference to manifest. Thus, heresy is by no means a wholesale evil; no, it makes us to appreciate and focus more on the marvellous beauty and brightness of the truth of the word.

But the messenger of God should not be hospitable to both. Only those who belong to the devil may peddle lies. It is thus of paramount importance for disciples to dissociate themselves from those who delight in confusing and confounding the little ones as proof of their faithfulness to the Lord.

This is a different matter from witch-hunting, which is alien to Christianity.

Exhortation, Meditation and Reflection.

The Lord says,

"Or how can you say to your brother, 'Brother, let me take out the speck that is in your eye', when you yourself don't see the log in your eye? Hypocrite! First take the log out of your eye, and then you will see clearly to take out the speck in your brother's eye." (Lk 6: 42 HSCB)

Orthodoxy and heresy are not matters for finger-pointing on persons.

Being born again

Everyone who announces the good news ought to be intent always at realizing the goal for our Christian formation. The essence of Christian formation is to have the mind of God, i.e., to be transformed in mind, heart, soul and spirit and be conformed to

God. Each has to become a soul seeking communion with, and submission to God.

Preaching the gospel from extraneous motives

Improper motive leads to undue emphasis and outright distortion and suppression of the true message – a thorn in the flesh it is in this age of misinformation and disinformation.

Preaching from subterranean motives leads to undue emphasis, scant attention to matters of grave concern and outright distortion of facts. The truth is suppressed by disinformation. It is as bad as blasphemy.

"To be sure, some preach Christ out of envy and strife, but others out of goodwill.

What does it matter? Just that in every way, whether out of false motives or true, Christ is proclaimed." (Phil 1: 15, 18 HCSB)

But, brothers and sisters, be watchful; because disinformation from ulterior motives frequently ends up proclaiming not Christ, but the antichrist; not salvation but doom, to its hearers.

"Many deceivers have gone out into the world;..." (2 Jn 1: 7 HCSB)

"Don't be led astray by... strange teachings..." (Heb 13: 9 HCSB)

Our exhortation

For our exhortation didn't come from error or impurity or an intent to deceive. (2 Thes 2: 3-4)

Reform can easily be hijacked by Satan

Whether anyone likes it or not, the devil will try to ensnare people out of the truth and away from obedience to God. (Gen 3: 1-5) Thus, apostasy exists as long as there is orthodoxy.

Exhortation, Meditation and Reflection

Don't take your zeal for the truth as a call for reform. First, establish that you have the sinews – a capacity to endure persecution (from the left or from the right); if you lack the call, you may end up destroying the very edifice you set out to renovate and you would more appropriately be called a destroyer rather than a builder. How could you resist the devil unless you are sent?

Remember, Jesus is a reformer (Mal 3: 3); but it takes two to tango; Judaism would not be reformed yet Jesus succeeded (in Christianity) but without the following of the rabbi!

Just as Jesus and His disciples were going out, "a demon – possessed man who was unable to speak was brought to Him. When the demon had been driven out, the man spoke. And the people were amazed, saying, 'Nothing like this has ever been seen in Israel!'

But the Pharisees said, 'He drives out demons by the ruler of the demons!'" (Matt 9: 32-34 HCSB)

"Cultural Blind spots"[1]

"2 Cor 4: 4: …blinded by the god of the present age."
Cultural blindness are like scales that obscure our vision to the truth of the word.

The Institution of human slavery, infanticide.

Onesimus means 'useful' in English. Philemon was the slave master.

"How can they take three slaves and sell them for six pigs?"

Consider the ethnic cleansing of the Third Reich… the Milad Massacre in Vietnam where thousands of lives were destroyed.

How can slavery be acceptable in its time and not recognised as reprehensible?

In a book on St Peter Claver and his work in 1600 in Colombia by Angel Sanpierra Morale quoted there was a passage in which a papal bull by Pope Nicholas V to the king:

"It is granted to… king of Portugal that he may claim for himself and his descendants any Saracens, kingdoms… any possessions that they may possess … and subject the aforesaid persons to perpetual slavery"

1: Fr Al-Leur, Daily Bread, op. cit. (redacted from the oral podcast).

Exhortation, Meditation and Reflection.

"John 8: 31 – unless we abide in the word, we may not be able to overcome such cultural blind spots which blind us from seeing as reprehensible such cultural practices of our time such as infanticide, all forms of abortion; euthanasia, etc."

Liberation and Salvation[1]

In his meditation on the above theme, which is really on the essence of truth, his holiness, Pope Emeritus, Benedict XVI has this to say:

"But what can liberate man?

Who liberates him and to what? Put even more simply, what is human freedom? Can man become free without truth – i.e., in falsehood?

Liberation is about the truth. Liberation without the truth will be a lie – will be deception and thus man's enslavement and man's ruin."

If we ever can make progress to grapple with the truth about the godhead – to know God, we must be committed to separating truth from lie; to demystify as many 'mysteries' as possible. In truth, we deal with certainty, which is far superior to uncertainty or assumption. This is how mankind has moved forward in our knowledge of the earth, sun and moon. Knowledge advances our faith, while ignorance our fear!

Reason is indispensable to wisdom and wisdom to discerning the truth. You cannot dispense with record and be wise, for the Scripture says, "thus, while revelations and visions cannot be queried or be subjected to human evaluation, there is a lot we can do before any such claims are accepted! Otherwise, we would be putting the cart before the horse. That is where reason comes handy. Experience has shown that visions or revelations may be mis-interpreted; the use of human language to describe heavenly matters may demand a mastery of language far above the ability of the visionary, which the subject may not adequately possess. Such interpretations can be challenged or even proved to be faulty, leading to wrong conclusions. Yet, with a rigorous application of the same reason, fresh vistas or truths that are unassailable may become manifest. Nothing is sacrosanct and unalterable about the truth.

1: Daily Meditation of Pope Benedict XVI

Exhortation, Meditation and Reflection.

We have got to learn to separate the truth from the myth; the message from the messenger. Liberate religion from the captivity of assumption/misinformation and superstition, then the truth will emerge. We know by reason that there is God; God is real, and this is confirmed by revelation. Who is afraid that age old beliefs may be smashed? That is for good, if it will thus unveil the truth, so let it be. The truth will set us free.

Faith will prosper and be fruitful when based on confident truth. Not only faith comes by grace, even reason and every other good gift comes to us (from God) by grace.

We can benefit from scholarship or research into the content, nature and dependability or validity of visions, apparitions, dreams and their limitations, if any. This becomes imperative because of fakes. Besides, we have evidence that these can be induced by use of herbs, meditations (yoga?), fasting or denial of food, mortification (asceticism) practices; prayer and faith. What is the relationship of trance to visions and dreams?

The scripture truculently enjoins us to seek God! We do this by due exercise of industry and diligence. Sometimes revelation comes as a reward for obedience and such diligence.

God's kingdom is the kingdom of light; but there is also another kingdom – the kingdom of darkness. Truth belongs to the kingdom of light; cynicism, doubt and denial to the kingdom of darkness. We have true or valid doctrines but so also are fake; we need reason to reveal the difference. How wonderful it would be if we can make ever efficacious supplications? Only the truth can lead us there. We want to be able to tap into God's wisdom, God's help in tackling human challenges, Jesus is the way, the truth and the life; He invites us 'Come to Me.' If we seek the truth we should be anxious to take advantage of that offer. But are we? Jesus says, 'Be One!' but we stay apart as separate islands, dishing out tendentious or opionated teachings about the truth. Many are comfortable with that also! Come off it. The truth is bitter, and many will rather listen to only what they want to hear.

Intellect in believing

1. "Now we know that You KNOW EVERYTHING and don't need anyone to question You. By this we believe that You came from God." (Jn 16: 30 HCSB)

Exhortation, Meditation and Reflection.

2. "And he went into synagogue and spoke boldly for three months, reasoning and persuading concerning the things of the kingdom of God." (Acts 19: 8 NKJV)

The Truth

"... Every fact must be established by the testimony of two or three witnesses."

"For we are not able to do anything against the truth, but only for the truth."

"Finally, brothers, rejoice. Become mature, be encouraged, be of the same mind, be at peace, and the God of love and peace will be with you."

(2 Cor 13: 1, 8, 11 HCSB)

On who has the final say in interpreting the Scripture

The Need

Secular authorities have long come to terms with the certainty that there will be misapprehension among persons on very important issues that ought to be clarified, for example, on the rights and duties between borrowers and lenders or even between husbands and wives! Thus, laws are promulgated, but there could be issues in the interpretation of such laws – hence the introduction of a supposedly free-from-bias judicial system.

The Arbiter

Who, then, can we trust to clarify to us everything about Christ's life and teaching?

We have, naturally, different schools of thought on the matter. Some say,

1. Individuals.

Your personal understanding (of scripture) should build the bulwark of your faith. "A man convinced against his will is of the same opinion still."[1]

But we are all learners; it is faster and surer to acquire knowledge if someone who is versed on the subject takes us through. Besides, in the case of irreconcilable differences with a fellow adherent of the faith, how do you win him over to you or you to him? It is important, that we remain in communion – isn't it?

2. The Church.

The magisterium of the church comes to our help. This accords with Jesus teaching on dispute resolution mechanism (Matt 18: 16-17).

Exhortation, Meditation and Reflection.

The church pontificates! You know we all – prophets/priests, monks, the religious and the faithful – constitute the body of Christ, the church; our leaders speak for us in one voice, in unanimity. Although some of us may be given to emotions, others to reason, still others to subjectivism, and others go for objective reality, the church is the referral body, the arbiter. Guided by the Holy Spirit, she establishes the fact – for the time being.

Yes, **'for the time being,'** because we gain deeper insight over time, and the church cannot afford to ignore glaring evidence that has become open in the future. Really, isn't that the core of our grouse with Judaism, that it would not accommodate any 'new' facts, even when it comes from God?

But if we must admit the truth, nobody can walk by other people's faith. To bear fruit, you must own the faith yourself! It is little comfort that the church had decreed what the faith should be. If, for now, you are not convinced, then you don't share in it, though you must accept it!

Hence, we the church, should listen to what the people are saying so we can clear some of their concerns and we must also listen to God, who speaks to the church through her members.

My take is this: let us tolerate (within the same body of Christ) persons with dissenting opinions on one or other issue of doctrine that is really not fundamental to the faith; that would not impugn the integrity of the faith or impinge negatively upon the obligations of the individual to God (and to man) and that would not make such individual unrighteous. If doing this enlarges our consensus base, so good! "We are stronger together!"[2]

"If we stand together, we shall rise together!"[2]

1:Alexander Pope

2:Mrs. Hilary Clinton, former US Senator, secretary of State and Presidential candidate (2016 election)

Exhortation, Meditation and Reflection.

On unity in faith and oneness in apostleship.

Apostle Paul, to the Galatians:

"… I want you to know, brothers, that the gospel preached by me is not based on human thought… but it came by a revelation from Jesus Christ."

"But when God who… called me… was pleased to reveal His Son… so that I could preach Him among the Gentiles, I did not immediately consult with anyone. I did not go up to Jerusalem to those who had become apostles before me…"

"Then after three years, I did go to Jerusalem to get to know Cephas… But I didn't see any of the other apostles except James…"

"Then after 14 years, I went up again to Jerusalem with Barnabas… I went up according to a revelation and persecuted? To them the gospel I teach…"

"… **false brothers smuggled in, who came secretly to spy… But we did not give up and submit to these people…**"

"Now from those recognised as important – they added nothing to me. On the contrary, they saw that I had been entrusted with the gospel for the uncircumcised, just as Peter was for the circumcised, since the One at work in Peter… was also at work in me…"

"When James, Cephas and John recognized as pillars, acknowledged the grace that had been given to me, they gave fellowship to me… agreeing that we should go to the Gentiles and they to the circumcised. They asked only that we would remember the poor, which I made every effort to do."

(Gal 1: 11-12, 15-16, 18-19; 2: 1-2, 4-7, 9-10 HCSB)

Let us – all Christians, but especially the leadership – put on our thinking caps. What does the above passage tell us about the necessity for a meeting of the minds on our understanding of our faith and on orthodoxy? What was Jesus' position thereon? Then, why are we acting differently?

Let us also remember the other side of the story as told in the Acts of the Apostles –

    i.   Saul, the persecutor: Acts 8:1
   ii.   The call of Saul (later baptized): Acts 9: 1-7, 15-18

    iii.   Saul (now Paul) first visit to Jerusalem and the role played by that holy man, Barnabas: Acts 9: 26-28

    iv.   Finally, the build-up of that enviable Antioch church: Acts 11: 22-24, 25-26.

Exhortation, Meditation and Reflection.

Let us discontinue fellowship with false brothers, but the faithful must first be together in fellowship.

A history of the division in the church

The origin of non-same fellowship sharing Christian bodies.

1. The Split: Disagreement over the addition of the Folioque (See Chapter 19).
2. Martin Luther and the protestant movement

The dispute

Martin, a German Roman Catholic priest disagreed with his colleague, his superiors and the church on the following issues (interalia):

- On power of the Pope to grant indulgences, Luther contradicted Johann Tetzel, a Dominican friar in 1517. He wrote to Tetzel's superior, Archbishop Albert of Mainz, sending alongside a copy of his 95 thesis which he entitled, "Disputation against scholastic theology."

Albert formally requested Rome to commence official proceedings to ascertain the works orthodoxy.

- Fund-raising for building the basilica of St. Peter.

Luther was opposed to it, querying why wouldn't "the pope, whose wealth today is greater than the wealth of the richest Crassus build with his own money rather than…"

- On papal primacy on theological interpretation, Luther contradicted, offering instead, *sola scriptura*, or the doctrine of the primacy of the bible.

On whose biblical interpretations are authoritative and the role of established theologians therewith, and the power of councils (such as the papal consistory of 1520 or the subsequent papal commission raised to examine Luther and which found his teachings heretical), Luther was for self-interpretation by the faithful and has this to say:

"…even general councils such as the council of Constance (1414-18) can be in error when they promulgate opinion on the faith."

Johann Eck, commenting on Luther's position as postulated at the Leipzlg public debate (1519) considered Luther's position to be identical with that of Jan Hus, which the council of Constance had declared heretical.

Exhortation, Meditation and Reflection.

- On the need for priestly celibacy, Luther described it as "the work of the Devil." He, himself got married to Katherine of Borg, a former nun and proselyte on June 13, 1525. The couple had five children.
- Luther disagreed with his co-travellers in the protestant movement he had precipitated at the Marburg Colloquy (Oct 1-4, 1529). For example, with H. Zwingli?on the real presence of the body and blood of Christ in the eucharist. Luther disagreed that Jesus was spiritually?present in the communion host but not physically present. Similarly, by 1523 Luther departed to go for? more radical reforms with other reformers like Thomas Murtzer?, Martin Bucer, Philipp Melanch Cho
- Luther's position on Anabaptists was that "They should be hanged as seditionists"

- On Jews – they "should be expelled and their synagogue burned."

Effort at resolution

Cajetan, head of Dominican order was assigned to examine Luther's teaching at Augsburg. Luther described him as "an evasive, obscure and unintelligible theologian."

Heretical not heretical: A papal consistory was raised in 1520 to examine Luther to give him opportunity to defend or renounce his teaching. This was followed by a papal commission on the same issue. The former found his teaching heretical, while the latter (consisting of important monastic orders) confirmed that Luther's propositions were "scandalous and offensive to pious ears" but that they were not heretical.

Luther showed no remorse. So, on June 15, 1520 Pope Leo issued the bull which formally charged that 41 sentences in Luther's writings were heretical.

Luther was given 60 days to recant and another 60 days to make a report thereof to Rome.

Luther's response was a tract which he entitled "Against the execrable bull of the anti-christ" And on December 10, 1520 Luther made a bonfire of a copy of the bull in the public gaze.

Failure of détente – Luther convicted a heretic.

On January 3, 1521 was published a papal bull – which declared Luther a heretic.

Exhortation, Meditation and Reflection.

Ordinarily, Luther should have been apprehended by the secular government of his residence as a condemned heretic. But Charles V, newly elected German king indicated he was not disposed to act on the conviction of a German without proper hearing. The formal hearing was held at Worms on March 6, 1521. Luther did not recant any of the 41 indictments. So, on May 25, 1521 Charles V signed the edict against Luther and he was placed into protective custody.

A keen observer[1] reflected on this scenario thus, "Luther, a single individual presumed to challenge 1,500 years of Christian theological consensus."

The split within the split.

All these led to a division in the Western Roman Catholic Church, with some supporting the church and others, Luther. In no time, the 'protestants' could not hold together extending into different folds such as Lutheranism, Calvinism, Anglican communion, Anabaptists and anti-trinitarians, etc. Thus, bringing to fulfilment the prophetic words of AlekseiStepanovichKhomiakov (ASK).

Who was Martin Luther?

A German priest, theologian (and reformer?). He celebrated his first mass in May 1507. He was one of two chosen by his colleagues to make a representation to Pope Julius II.

He petitioned the theology faculty of the University of Erfurt to confer him a doctorate in theology. (Granted ultimately on their behalf by the university of Whitten burg in 1512). He later precipitated the protestants' movement that queried or offered an alternative reformation of age-old Christian beliefs and tradition.

After he had been formally declared a heretic and was placed in protective custody, he translated the New Testament into German language.

In 1539 Philip of Hesse (Landgrave) secretly married his wife's lady-in-waiting, with Luther's tacit support. It created a bigamy issue.

1: Dutch humanist Desiderius Erasmus.

Exhortation, Meditation and Reflection.

Before the revolution that Luther's protest ushered in no individual, but only the church, could found new Christian worship centres. Even today, most professional have found it necessary to restrict the practice of their profession to duly certified members. That way, the members of the public are protected from quacks and the reputation of the profession itself is safeguarded.

Christianity in the world today – an anomie.

The break continues till today. It has become the new norm. In many countries many religious people found their own churches in just the same way as secular clubs are formed, but often more frequently. Today, in Nigeria alone, there are more than 3,000 autocephalous Christian worship centres.Someone may ask, so then, what is wrong with that? Everything; nothing is right about it!

Orthodoxy, Protestantism and growth of free churches

"Not everyone should be teachers," lest the less informed among us may "cause others to stumble," even if unintentionally. The situation foists doubt on the flock instead of faith; weakness of the body of Christ, instead of strength. A lack of direction replaces purposiveness in Christian evangelism – i.e., growth by objectives (GBO) – salvation, is replaced with growth by greed (GBG). This shows off by forsaking the true path (the kingdom of God) for earthly glory. Many of these churches are not attentive to the Holy Spirit, but listen to Satan! Righteousness recedes; mass apostasy, prophesied, becomes increasingly unpreventable. As denominations flourish, growth in the knowledge of God stagnates.

Break-away occurs every second from existing mother churches. Is there anything we can do to avert this disaster – this binary fission?

The way forward

First, we can stop focusing on individuals; from henceforth our focus should be on institutions – from heretics to heretical institutions – institutions which do not qualify for the appellation, 'Christian.' That way, we would be separating the grain from the chaff and impeding the precocious growth of the weed among the wheat.

Why should anybody be killed by man (warfare apart)? Remember, "thou shall not kill."

Exhortation, Meditation and Reflection.

Murdering individuals for holding personal views not congruent withsociety's is hardly a valid exception. Besides, such religious killing tends to legitimatize the killing of pious people by demonic regimes. Struggling Christian entities ought to be assisted to stand firm; fakes, should be shown the way out – through denial of fellowship with them.

Like Luther, many of us suffer from some idiosyncrasies. We should learn to tolerate and accommodate one another. Perhaps, John Wesley's Methodists may then have remained an ecclesiola in ecclesia in the Anglican church, strengthening the latter, particularly in the Americas.

Perhaps there are many more lessons to learn from history, if we are so disposed to.

The dividers are divided: The Anglican church succumbs to a split

If Christianity had walked away from Judaism, because the latter would not absorb reform, the splinter groups that emerged from the crack in the Western Roman Catholic Church themselves underwent division atomistically for different causes. Western Catholicism broke into pieces because of the disrespect for duly constituted authority. The splinter groups emerging, like the Anglican Communion, could not hold together because of one or other of the aforementioned reasons.

In the case of John Wesley's[1]methodism, he was a full-time cleric of the Anglican communion until the end of his life. He did not set out to oppose that authority, or to create a new church, but he was zealous for the faith – for Christ. Split eventually occurred because there was no informal channel of communication between the echelons of the Anglican church, between the priests and laity and the higher ecclesiastics. Today, some churches hold synods which meet periodically; through its auspices various members of the church can talk to each other about their concerns on the faith – the priests, the religious and the lay faithful. That way, the church had ceased to be looked at as that of the pastor but as "our church."

1: John Wesley, 17
Exhortation, Meditation and Reflection.
Wesley's charisms

The primitivist motif:

Like in the early Christian community, Wesley's interest was to deepen the faith of believers as part of renewal of that old fervour.

Free (or believers') church:

Denominational allegiance is anti-thetical to that goal. Consequently, it is understandable therefore, that Wesley's goal was "forming a genuine people of God within the Anglican institutional church."

Nevertheless, one does not need to be an Anglican or a Methodist to be admitted into membership: "for their union with us we require no unity in opinion."

Discipline.

Wesley operated on the belief that the church must exercise discipline on a covenant commitment to Christian values as expected of a Christian community – to live and maintain the values of the kingdom of God in an inclement cultural environment "to be a Christian in a deteriorating hedonistic society."

To him, the church needs a structure based on norms of community discipline and mission. Thus, in 1748 Wesley reduced the Bristol society membership from 900 to 730. Some of the reasons for this were irregular attendance, wife-beating, etc.

All members were, of course, accountable to him personally (through their leaders).

He recognised the spiritual dimension of the church beyond that of a secular club; "it is a sacramental community." He postulated that "discipline has the relationship to justification that works have to faith…"

Missionary zeal:

Wesley's first love to build a genuine people of God led him into forming little bands of God seekers. He started from the street – from the Fetter lane society established in 1738, to the Newcastle-upon-Tyne (Sandgatestreet) open air preaching of May 30, 1742. To farther deepen penetration in evangelism he formed his itinerant band of travelling lay preachers. Ultimately, it led to the planting of his Methodist societies and church in America, the then new world. The appointment of local presbyters became insistent to enhance control beyond what he could accomplish from far away England.

Exhortation, Meditation and Reflection.

Who Wesley was

He was an Anglican clergyman and founder of the Methodist church which became about the largest "free church" in the protestant tradition.

For him "church" stands for believers in Christ thus, under-playing or denying the hierarchical structure as an essence. To him 'church unity' is fostered by the Christian Koinonia in the Holy Spirit. Apostolicity meant, "the succession of apostolic doctrine in those… faithful to the Apostolic witness."

His ecclesiology: "In religion, I am for as few innovations as possible," the first century Christian communities were his model.

Prevenient grace: He believed that on their own, human beings could not take the ………. smallest step toward God; but God's grace was prevenient.

Activism: He believed that the struggle for social justice sprang from the Bible – by building a community that was faithful to the scriptures.

Glossary

Bible References - Abbreviations Used

Old Testament		Old Testament	
Gen	Genesis	Nah	Nahum
Ex	Exodus	Hab	Habakkuk
Lev	Leviticus	Zep	Zephaniah
Num	Numbers	Hag	Haggai
Dt	Deuteronomy	Mal	Malachi
Jos	Joshua		
Jdg	Judges		
Rut	Ruth	**New Testament**	
1 Sam`	1 Samuel	Matt or Mt	Matthew
2 Sam	2 Samuel	Mk	Mark
I Kgs	1 Kings	Lk	Luke
2 Kgs	2 Kings	Jn	John
1 Chr	1 Chronicles	Acts	Acts of the Apostles
2 Chr	2 Chronicles	Rom	Romans
Ezr	Ezra	1 Cor	1 Corinthians
Neh	Nehemiah	2 Cor	2 Corinthians
Tob	Tobit	Gal	Galatians
Jdt	Judita	Eph	Ephesians
Est	Esther	Phil	Philippians
1 Mac	1 Maccabees	Col	Colossians
2 Mac	2 Maccabees	1 Thes	1 Thessalonians
Jb	Job	2 Thes	2 Thessalonians
Ps	Psalms	1 Tim	1 Timothy
Prov	Proverbs	2 Tim	2 Timothy
Eccl	Ecclesiastes	Tit	Titus

Song	Songs of Solomon	Phle	Philemon
Wis	Wisdom	Heb	Hebrews
Sir	Sirach (Ben),orEcclesiasticus	Js	James
Isa	Isaiah	1 Pt	1 Peter
Jer	Jeremiah	2 Pt	2 Peter
Lam	Lamentations	1 Jn	1 John
Bar	Baruch	2 Jn	2 John
Ezk	Ezekiel	3 Jn	3 John
Dan	Daniel	Jud	Jude
Hos	Hosea	Rev	Revelation
Jl	Joel		
Am	Amos		
Ob	Obadiah		
Jon	Jonah		
Mic	Micah		

Versions frequently used.

Unless otherwise indicated, the Bible passages quoted in this book are from the Holman Christian Standard Bible (HCSB), Holman Bible Publishers, Nashville, Tennessee © 2009.Other versions frequently cited are:

Good News Bible (Catholic Edition) in Septuagint order (GNBDK);New American Bible Revised Edition (NABRE);Lectionary for Mass in the USA (at other times for mass in UK); New King James Version (NKJV), New Revised Standard Version, Catholic Interconfessional(NRSV-CI) © 1989 (National Council of Churches of Christ in the USA).

Excerpts are also quoted from other versions not mentioned above, but occurless frequently, e.g. from the Liturgy of Hours (L of H), etc.